Praise for *Your Divine Birthright*

This book is an informative book to help new Christians. Foundational truths are presented in a systematic and easy to read format. Pastor's should give a copy to every new born believer. It will assist them in their spiritual journey.

> —Pastor Roger Hunt, Poplar Assembly Church, Fort Peck Indian Reservation, Montana

We have finished translating the book into Tagalog and are now using it in our new believer's class.

> —Jeffrey Pessina, Director of Philippine Frontline Ministries

I like the way this book keeps pointing me back to my Bible.

> —Bud Braaten, 82 year old Montana Cowboy

This book reveals the truth of Christ and I am encouraged by it.

> —John Atchico, Native American Shawnee Elder

This is a wonderful book that establishes the basic foundation every Christian believer needs to be sucessful in their walk of faith. It is easy to read, powerful, and fits in every society. It reveals the love, purpose and power of Christ and opens the door to "the life more abundant" Jesus promises those who follow him.

—Ronnie Binas, director of Lift Jesus Higher International, Bacolod City, Negros Island, Philippines

Your Divine Birthright

Your Divine Birthright

{JIM O'CONNOR}

TATE PUBLISHING & Enterprises

Published by Tate Publishing & Enterprises, LLC
127 E. Trade Center Terrace | Mustang, Oklahoma 73064 USA
1.888.361.9473 | www.tatepublishing.com

Tate Publishing is committed to excellence in the publishing industry. The company reflects the philosophy established by the founders, based on Psalm 68:11,
"The Lord gave the word and great was the company of those who published it."

Book design copyright © 2013 by Tate Publishing, LLC. All rights reserved.
Cover design by Kellie Southerland
Interior design by Stefanie Rooney

Published in the United States of America

ISBN: 978-1-62854-806-8
Religion, Christian Life, Spiritual Growth
13.07.12

Acknowledgments

I want to humbly thank the Lord for all he has done in my life and the grace he has shown me in writing this book. I also want to thank everyone who has helped me and prayed for me during the process.

Table of Contents

Introduction

If Jesus Christ said, "Greater things than I do will you do if you believe in me," then how do I get there? If he also said all things are possible to those who believe, then what conclusion does this bring us to? For me, it causes me to stubbornly refuse to believe God's best is a disciple who will settle for less than the fullness of the life in Christ that becomes ours once we are born-again. This relationship with Jesus Christ will free us from sin, deliver us from our weakness, and release the power of God to us and through us. This relationship is an ongoing process that calls us further and further from tradition and religion and deeper and deeper into Christ.

If God is calling you to a new lifestyle as his disciple, you are going to have to look beyond your religious beliefs to a new life in Christ; a life of more than yourself, as you live in a relationship with him.

In this new place of relationship, all things are

possible for you as a person. This is not only true for you and me; it is also God's calling and privilege for everyone. The Bible declares to us the normal thing in God's plan for one of his children is for them to become mature, attaining to the whole measure of the fullness of Christ.

You need to understand that God loves you and that Jesus Christ died and shed his blood for your sins. If you will believe and accept this, you can live where all things are possible to those who believe. The beginning is to believe in Christ's reality and power. From this point, you must move on to live and release it. The old carnal man must be laid aside as you become the powerful spiritual vessel God intends.

God is calling you to walk with him in a correct personal relationship through Jesus Christ. I pray you will move beyond simple mental agreement in his teaching. Go past religious experience. Break the bondage of traditions. Enter into this living relationship of power and abundant lifestyle. Say to God and to yourself, *I want all you have for me Lord.*

I pray that you will come to know not only the theory, but also the reality and power of the resurrection of Jesus Christ!

Welcome

Once you have surrendered yourself to Jesus and have asked to be forgiven your sins; you must then invite him into your heart and ask him to make you new.

I pray for you as the Apostle Paul prayed for the converts in the early Christian church. My desire for you is reflected so well in his prayer found in Colossians 1:9–14.

> So ever since we first heard about you, we have kept on praying and asking God to help you understand what he wants you to do; asking him to make you wise about spiritual things; and asking that the way you live will always please the Lord and honor him, so that you will always be doing good, kind things for others, while all the time you are learning to know God better and better. We are praying, too, that you will be filled with his mighty, glorious strength so that you can keep going no matter what happens; always full

of the joy of the Lord, and always thankful to the Father who has made us fit to share all the wonderful things that belong to those who live in the kingdom of light. For he has rescued us out of the darkness and gloom of Satan's kingdom and brought us into the kingdom of his dear son, who bought freedom with his blood and forgave us all our sins.

Please come with me as we continue to know Jesus and become his disciple.

Jesus

One time in my travels, I met the nicest of fellows. We sat together in the airport waiting for our planes to arrive. He was interesting to talk to and was most delightful to be with. Time passed quickly and much too soon it was time for us to continue our individual journeys. As nice as this man was, I did not change my plans or purpose to follow him. To this very day, I don't know any more about him than I did the day we met for a moment as our paths crossed in that airport.

As wondrous as it is when you ask Jesus into your heart, you then have a decision to make. Will you change your plans, cancel your schedule, and follow him? Only when your answer is a definite yes will you truly be ready to press on in developing your relationship with Jesus Christ.

> If anyone wishes to come after me, let him deny himself, and take up his cross, and follow me. For

whoever wishes to save his life shall lose it; but whoever loses his life for my sake and the gospels, shall save it.

Mark 8:34–35, (NAS)

Take my yoke upon you and learn from me, for I am gentle and lowly in heart, and you will find rest for your souls. For my yoke is easy and my burden is light.

Matthew 11:29–30, (NKJV)

I know a woman who experienced a terrible thing in her life. She married a fine young man who was in the Navy. She felt she knew him completely. After fifteen years, she was still secure in believing the man she married was the person she knew and believed in. One day, she went to the mailbox and discovered a bill for some dental work concerning their teenage daughter. The age was right, but the name wasn't. In looking into the matter, she found that her husband had another woman and another daughter the same age as theirs. He was not who she thought he was. As terrible as this was to her and her life, it will be far more tragic at the end of our lives if we follow the Jesus of our beliefs and not the true Jesus of the Scripture. To develop a correct and intimate relationship with Jesus Christ, there are pure truths in the Bible we must believe to establish the foundation upon which we stand with power and build our life together with him.

The Bible reveals Jesus as Eternal God who lived as sinless man and is the Savior.

As eternal God, he is one with God the Father. As a man, he lived a sinless life on earth, died on the cross, rose from the dead, and ascended into heaven. As the Savior, he is the one and only way for us to come to God. We must believe this truth if we are to live as a Christian disciple. If we see Jesus as anything less than one with the Father (God), or other than living as flesh and blood as we are (Man), or if we believe there is any other way to God outside of Jesus Christ (Savior), we will not be capable of relating to God the way he expects us to.

We need to see Jesus as *one* with God. In Isaiah 9:6–7 (spoken prophetically over 600 years before the birth of Jesus) we read:

> For unto us a child is born, unto us a son is given: and the government shall be upon his shoulder: and his name shall be called Wonderful Counselor, The Mighty God, The Everlasting Father, the Prince of Peace. Of the increase of his government and peace there shall be no end. (KJV)

Following are some other important scriptures regarding the issue of Jesus being one with God (the divinity of Christ).

> In the beginning was the Word and the Word was with God, and the Word was God. He was in the beginning with God. All things were made through him, and without him nothing was made that was made. In him was life, and the life was the light of men ... That was the true light, which gives light to every man coming into the world.
> John 1:1–4, 9 (NKJV)

I and my Father are one.

John 10:30 (KJV)

But unto the Son he saith, Thy throne, O God is forever and ever:

Hebrews 1:8 (KJV)

He is the image of the invisible God, the firstborn over all creation. For by him all things were created: things in heaven and on earth, visible and invisible, whether thrones or powers or authorities; all things were created by him and for him. He is before all things, and in him all things hold together. And he is the head of the body, the church; he is the beginning and the firstborn from among the dead, so that in everything he might have the supremacy.

Colossians 1:15–18 (NIV)

The simple truth is this. Jesus was not created; He is the Creator! We see from these scriptures that Jesus was in the beginning with the Father and (as we read in Isaiah 9:6, John 1:1, and Hebrews 1:8) he is one with God.

The scriptures teach us Jesus came to earth and became a man.

Who being in very nature God, did not consider equality with God something to be grasped, but made himself nothing, taking the very nature of a servant, being made in human likeness. And being found in appearance as a man he humbled himself and became obedient unto death—even death on a cross! Therefore, God exalted him to the highest place and gave him the name that is above every name, that at the name of Jesus every knee should bow, in heaven and on earth, and every tongue confess that Jesus Christ is Lord, to the glory of God the Father.

Philippians 2:6–11, (NIV)

He was in the world, and the world was made through him, and the world did not know him … And the word became flesh and dwelt among us, and we beheld his glory, the glory of the only begotten of the Father, full of grace and truth.

John 1:10–14 (NKJV)

He came to earth and was born of a virgin.

All this took place to fulfill what the Lord has said through the prophet: "The virgin will be with child and will give birth to a son, and they will call him Immanuel" which means, "God with us."

Matthew 1:22–23 (NIV)

Then said Mary unto the Angel, "how shall this be, seeing I know not a man?" And the Angel answered and said to her, "The Holy Ghost shall come upon thee, and the power of the Highest shall overshadow thee; therefore also that holy thing which shall be born of thee shall be called the Son of God."

Luke 1:34–35, (KJV)

He lived a sinless life.

For we do not have a high priest who is unable to sympathize with our weaknesses, but we have one who has been tempted in every way, just as we are—yet without sin.

Hebrews 4:15 (NIV)

He revealed the love of the Father.

For God so loved the world that he gave his only begotten son, that whosoever believes in him should not perish, but have everlasting life.

John 3:16 (NKJV)

"How God anointed Jesus of Nazareth with the Holy Spirit and with power, who went about doing good and healing all who were oppressed by the devil, for God was with him."

Acts 10:38 (NKJV)

He was crucified and died.

And when they were come to the place, which is called Calvary, there they crucified him.

Luke 23:33 (KJV)

And it was the third hour, and they crucified him. And the superscription of his accusation was written over, THE KING OF THE JEWS.

Mark 15:25–26 (KJV)

This man went to Pilate and asked for the body of Jesus. Then Pilate commanded the body to be given him. When Joseph had taken the body, he wrapped it in a clean linen cloth, and laid it in his new tomb which he had hewn out of rock; and he rolled a large stone against the door of the tomb, and departed.

Matthew 27:58–60 (NKJV)

He rose from the dead.

And the angel answered and said unto the women, fear not ye; for I know that ye seek Jesus, which was crucified. He is not here: for he is risen, as he said. Come see the place where the Lord lay. And go quickly, and tell his disciples that he is risen from the dead;

Matthew 28:5–7 (KJV)

He appeared to his disciples and many other people after he arose from the dead. One time, he appeared to a crowd of over five hundred people. Then one day, in the presence of his disciples, he ascended "in a cloud" into heaven.

And that he was buried, and that he rose again the third day according to the Scripture: And that he was seen of Cephas, then of the twelve: After that, he was seen of above five hundred brethren at once; of whom the greater part remain unto this present, but some are fallen asleep. After that, he was seen of James; then of all the apostles. And last of all he was seen of me also, as of one born out of due time.

1 Corinthians 15:4–9 (KJV)

And it came to pass, while he blessed them, he was parted from them, and carried up into heaven.

Luke 24:51 (KJV)

So after the Lord had spoken unto them, he was received up into heaven, and sat on the right hand of God.

Mark 16:19 (KJV)

But because Jesus lives forever, he has a permanent priesthood. Therefore, he is able to save completely those who come to God through him because he always lives to intercede for them.

Hebrews 7:24–25, (NIV)

The scriptures also teach us Jesus will return again at the end of this age to judge the world of sin and forever establish his kingdom.

In my Father's house there are many mansions: if it were not so, I would have told you. I go to prepare a place for you. And if I go and prepare a place for you, I will come again, and receive you unto myself; that where I am, there ye may be also.

John 14:2–3 (KJV)

But every man in his own order: Christ the firstfruits; afterward they that are Christ's at his coming. Then cometh the end, when he shall have delivered up the kingdom to God, even the Father; when he shall have put down all rule and all authority and power. For he must reign, till he hath put all enemies under his feet.

1 Corinthians 15:23–25 (KJV)

And the seventh angel sounded; and there were great voices in heaven, saying, the kingdoms of this world are become the kingdoms of our Lord, and of his Christ; and he shall reign forever and ever.

Revelations 11:15 (KJV)

For we shall all stand before the judgment seat of Christ. For it is written: "As I live, says the LORD, Every knee shall bow to Me, and every tongue shall confess to God." So then each of us shall give an account of himself to God.

Romans 14:10–12 (NKJV)

We need to separate ourselves from those who claim to be Christians if they preach and teach a different Jesus than the one clearly seen in the Holy Scriptures.

Let's now look at Jesus as Savior. We will see he is not one of many ways to get to God, but he is the only way.

Jesus answered, "I am the way and the truth and the life. No one comes to the Father except through me…"

John 14:6 (NIV)

For there is one God, and one mediator between God and men, the man Christ Jesus;

1 Timothy 2:5 (KJV)

To wit God was in Christ, reconciling the world unto himself, not imputing their trespasses unto them;

2 Corinthians 5:19 (KJV)

And from Jesus Christ, who is the faithful witness, and the firstborn from the dead, and the prince of the kings of the earth. Unto him that loved us, and washed us from our sins in his own blood.

Revelation 1:5 (KJV)

And you being dead in your trespasses and the uncircumcision of your flesh, he has made alive together with him. Having forgiven you all trespasses. Having wiped out the handwriting of requirement which was contrary to us. And he has taken it out of the way, having nailed it to the cross. Having disarmed principalities and powers, he made a public spectacle of them, triumphing over them in it.

Colossians 2:13–15 (NKJV)

Surely he hath born our griefs, and carried our sorrows: yet we did esteem him stricken, smitten of God, and afflicted. But he was wounded for our transgressions; he was bruised for our iniquities: the chastisement of our peace was upon him; and with his stripes we are healed.

Isaiah 53:4–5 (KJV)

So Christ was once offered to bear the sins of many; and unto them that look for him shall he appear the second time without sin unto salvation.

Hebrews 9:28 (KJV)

But if we walk in the light, as he is in the light, we have fellowship one with another, and the blood of Jesus Christ his Son cleanseth us from all sin.

1 John 1:7 (KJV)

We see how God became man through Jesus (and the Word became flesh and dwelt among us), and while he was on this earth as sinless man, he became our healing, saving Savior (and through him to reconcile to himself all things ... by making peace through his blood on the cross).

Jesus isn't religion; he is reality. I found this out as a young man. I was drunk with wine for the first time when I was twelve years old. I was arrested for being intoxicated in public when I was fifteen. I stood before a judge when I was sixteen for hitting a man with a car door and leaving him in the ditch beside the road. I was wicked and angry. I have been in jail and other places where there is no peace. When I was twenty-three, I knelt alone in my bedroom and asked Jesus if he was real. That night I met the King of kings and Lord of lords. He heard me as I called to him. He took my sin and shame from me by his blood and he saved me. Jesus is more than fact and history: he is alive! There is no other religion known to man where we find a personal relationship with God. He stands at the door of our heart and knocks and to those who will open to him; he will come in and fellowship with them.

As a disciple, we will encounter many who do not have a proper understanding of who Jesus is. Some believe he was a good man and try to follow his example. Some say he was one of the great prophets who God has sent through the ages. Some say he was an angel created by God and sent to show mankind love. Some even go so far as to believe he was the first created being in the plan of God and now brings salvation to man. Those who believe these things simply have an incomplete and incorrect understanding of who Jesus really is.

The Bible clearly states Jesus was and is one with God. He was in the beginning with God and was God. He was born of a virgin, became man, shed his blood at the cross, rose from the dead, and now sits at the right hand of the Father, praying for us. One day soon, he will return to reign as Lord of lords and King of kings forever!

> "I am alpha and omega," says the Lord, "who is and who was and who is to come the Almighty."
> Revelation 1:8 (NAS)

> Do not be afraid I am the first and the last, and the living One; and I was dead, and behold, I am alive forevermore, and I have the keys of death and of Hades.
> Revelation 1:17–18 (NAS)

Today he dwells in our hearts by faith! Praise his name!

This is a very brief introduction to this vast and wonderful study of the person of Jesus Christ and the relationship we are called to with him. I pray this will encourage you to move forward in a lifelong love and devotion to your newfound Savior and Lord.

Let's pray before we go on:

Jesus I ask you to forgive me and save me. I believe that you love me and want a relationship with me. I ask you to make yourself known to me and help me. I now surrender all to you. In your name, Jesus, I pray. Amen.

Faith

Faith is something we don't think about much before we find Jesus. We might have faith (believe) in ourselves to accomplish our goals. We might have faith (believe) in objects to be strong enough to maintain the pressure we place against them, like sitting in a chair. This is natural faith we have as we live.

I want to talk to you about faith in God. Our life in God begins when we place our faith in Jesus Christ and in what the Bible tells us about ourselves and about our relationship with him.

> For all have sinned and fall short of the glory of God, and are justified freely by his grace through the redemption that came by Christ Jesus.
>
> Romans 3:23–24 (NIV)

> For the wages of sin is death, but the gift of God is eternal life in Christ Jesus our Lord.
>
> Romans 6:23 (NIV)

27

> The word is near you; it is in your mouth and in your heart, that is, the word of faith we are proclaiming: that if you confess with your mouth and believe in your heart that God raised him from the dead, you will be saved. For it is with your heart you believe and are justified, and it is with your mouth that you confess and are saved.
>
> Romans 10:8–10 (NIV)

> And without faith it is impossible to please God, because anyone who comes to him must believe that he exists and that he rewards those who earnestly seek him.
>
> Hebrews 11:6 (NIV)

We begin our relationship with God through our faith (belief).

Once we realize we are alienated from God, we must repent and accept Jesus dying on the cross, and the shedding of his blood as payment for our sin. When we do this and confess our salvation to others, we can know a life with God. At the time of receiving Jesus into our heart, we are born-again. His life becomes a part of us as we live in relationship with him. This divine influence is spoken of as grace in the Scripture.

> For by grace are ye saved through faith, and not of yourselves: it is the gift of God: not of works, lest any man should boast.
>
> Ephesians 2:8–9, (KJV)

> Therefore being justified by faith, we have peace with God through our Lord Jesus Christ: By

whom also we have access by faith into this grace
wherein we stand and rejoice in hope of the glory
of God.

Romans 5:1–2 (KJV)

It is by faith we receive Jesus Christ and begin
our relationship with God. It is also by faith we live
in relationship with him. In Hebrews 11:1–2, we read
that faith is being sure of what we hope for and being
certain of that we do not see and that the ancients
were commended for this. It tells us in 2 Corinthians
5:7, as Christians we walk (live) by faith and not by
sight. We live knowing what we cannot see is more
real and of greater authority and eternal value than
what we can behold with our natural eyes. This is of
such importance it is repeated four times in Scripture.

We read in Habakkuk, 2:4, Romans 1:17, Galatians 3:11 and Hebrews 10:38 "the just shall live by his
faith" (KJV). So we see that all we do from start to finish with God must be by faith. We read in Romans
14:23, "For whatsoever is not of faith is sin" (KJV).

True faith brings us to be obedient to God and
his Word. This opens us up to a life of relationship
with God and in this relationship our faith releases
his divine presence and power into our circumstances
and the affairs of this world. I remember a little song
I heard one time:

Got any rivers you think are un-crossable?
Got any mountains you can't tunnel through?
God specializes in things thought impossible
There is nothing my Father can't do!

But in him it has always been "yes." For no matter how many promises God has made, they are "Yes" in Christ.

2 Corinthians 1:20 (NIV)

God said it this way to Abraham's wife Sarah:

Is anything too hard for the LORD?

Genesis 18:14 (NKJV)

To the prophet Jeremiah the Lord said:

I am the LORD the God of all mankind. Is anything too hard for me?

Jeremiah 32:27 (NKJV)

Call unto me, and I will answer thee, and show thee great and mighty things, which thou knowest not.

Jeremiah 33:3 (KJV)

The angel that appeared to the Virgin Mary said:

For nothing is impossible with God ...

Luke 1:37 (NIV)

Jesus himself said to those who were listening to him:

Everything is possible for him who believes.

Mark 9:23 (NIV)

And all things you ask in prayer, believing, you shall receive.

Matthew 21:22 (NAS)

"Have faith in God," Jesus answered, "I tell you the truth, if anyone says to this mountain, Go, throw yourself into the sea, and does not doubt in his heart, but believes that what he says will happen, it will be done for him. Therefore I tell you, whatever you ask for in prayer, believe that you have received it, and it will be yours."

Mark 11:22–24 (NIV)

"I tell you the truth, anyone who has faith in me will do what I have been doing. He will do even greater things than these, because I am going to my Father. And I will do whatever you ask in my name, so that the Son may bring glory to the Father. You may ask me for anything in my name, and I will do it."

John 14:12–14 (NIV)

This is true!

When Peter saw this, he said to them: "Men of Israel, why does this surprise you? Why do you stare at us as if by our own power or godliness we had made this man walk? By faith in the name of Jesus, this man whom you see and know was made strong. It is Jesus' name and the faith that comes through him that has given this complete healing to him, as you can all see.

Acts 3:12–16 (NIV)

I hope you are beginning to understand that faith in Jesus Christ opens up a whole New World as we walk in relationship with him. I want to encourage you to be bold in your faith, believing all things are possible as you walk with God.

New Birth

Are you wondering about the term *born-again?* I will help you understand this, because I, too, pondered what it meant after I became a Christian. This simple term has confounded the wisest of men and has been ridiculed by unbelievers for centuries. I assure you, however, it is not foolish, nor is it confusing once you understand it.

Let's look at the first recorded encounter between Jesus and someone he spoke to concerning this matter. In the third chapter of the Gospel of John, we read about Nicodemus, a ruler of the Jews and a Pharisee who came to Jesus by night. He was a man who had been observing the life and ministry of our Lord. Nicodemus opened the conversation by confessing he was sure Jesus had come from God, because he was convinced no one could do all the miracles Jesus was doing apart from the Creator. Instead of replying to what Nicodemus said, Jesus began talking about being born again, saying: "Most assuredly, I say to you, unless one is born again, he cannot see the kingdom of God" (John 3:3, NKJV). This made about as much sense to Nicodemus then as it did to us the first time we heard it. Not understanding what Jesus was saying, Nicodemus asked how a man could be born a second time once he was already grown. Again, instead of responding to the question in the way Nicodemus expected, Jesus simply continued:

> Most assuredly, I say to you, unless one is born of water and the Spirit, he cannot enter the kingdom of God. That which is born of the flesh is flesh, and that which is born of the Spirit is spirit.
>
> John 3:5–6 (NKJV)

As we study this, we can see Jesus is saying we not only need to be born as a baby to our natural parents, but we also need to be born of the Spirit unto God. This is why Jesus said, "born again." We read in John 1:12–13:

> But as many as received him, to them gave he power to become the sons of God, even to them that believe on his name: Which were born, not of blood, nor of the will of the flesh, nor of the will of man, but of God. (KJV)

To understand this better, we need to go back to the first book in the Bible, Genesis, where we read about the creation of the first man, Adam:

Let us make man in our image, in our likeness.
So God created man in his image; in the image of
God ... He created him; male and female he created them ... the Lord God formed man from the
dust of the ground and breathed into his nostrils
the breath of life; and man became a living being.

Genesis 1:26–27 (NIV)

We read where God, having made man and
woman, then planted a garden to the east, and there
in the Garden of Eden, he placed Adam and Eve.
With them God placed all kinds of trees, of which
two are mentioned by name; "the Tree of Life" and
the "Tree of the Knowledge of Good and Evil." he
then instructed Adam and Eve; they were free to eat
from all the trees in the garden except for the Tree of
the Knowledge of Good and Evil.

Concerning this tree, God said, "But of the Tree
of the Knowledge of Good and Evil, thou shalt not
eat of it for the day that thou eatest thereof thou
shalt surely die" (Genesis 2:17 KJV).

We see in the beginning, God created man with
the power of choice; or in other words, Adam had
the sovereignty within himself to choose his own
destiny. He had the sovereignty to choose the Tree of
Life and live and have dominion within the garden,
he also had the sovereignty to disobey and forfeit
God's intention for him. The scripture goes on to say
man chose of his own freewill to eat of the Tree of
the Knowledge of Good and Evil. As a result of this
decision, he fell from his glorious state of purity and
obedience to a state of disobedience and guilt.

So the Lord God banished him from the Garden of Eden to work the ground from which he had been taken. After he drove the man out, he placed on the east side of the Garden of Eden a cherubim and a flaming sword flashing back and forth to guard the way to the Tree of Life. Adam lay with his wife Eve and she became pregnant and gave birth to Cain. She said, with the help of the Lord I have brought forth a man.

Genesis 3:23–4:1 (NIV)

God then put them out of the garden. Adam and Eve went on to have children and live many more years. *Wait a minute…* I thought we just read how God said the day they ate of the tree's fruit, they would surely die. Yes, we did read this, and yes, they did die. As we read on in Genesis chapter four, we see Adam and Eve continued to live in the flesh, to have children, and become the progenitors of all people. So we see this death wasn't physical. They continued to think, reason, and show emotion; so we see their death wasn't in the soul. Then how did they die? This death was a spiritual death.

The spiritual death caused by sin not only separated Adam and Eve from God, it also has separated everyone who has been born after them. Note what we read in Romans 5:12–19 (NKJV).

Therefore, just as through one man sin entered the world, and death through sin, and thus death spread to all men, because all sinned. But the free gift is not like the offense. For if by the one man's offense many died, much more the grace of God and the gift by the grace of the one man, Jesus Christ, abounded to man. And the gift is not like that which came through the one who sinned; for the judgment that came from one offense resulted in condemnation, but the free gift that came from many offenses resulted in justification. For if by the one man's offenses death reined through the one; much more those who receive abundance of grace and the gift of righteousness will reign in life through the One, Jesus Christ. Therefore, as through one man's offense, judgment came to all men, resulting in condemnation; even so through one man's righteous act the free gift came to all men, resulting in justification of life. For as by one man's disobedience, many were made sinners; so also by one man's obedience, many will be made righteous.

God made him who had no sin to be sin for us, so that in him we might become the righteousness of God.

2 Corinthians 5:21 (NIV)

So you see we all are partakers of the fall of Adam and need to be redeemed from our fallen state. For this reason, Jesus came to die on the cross so that he could redeem us back to God. This is why Jesus said, "You must be born-again." The dead spirit man within us must be born-again in order to live for God and to have fellowship with God. Without being born-again, we may be alive physically, but spiritually we will remain separated from God. We will all live eternally, but only those who experience this new birth through Jesus Christ will be in heaven with him.

> Giving thanks to the Father who has qualified us to be partakers of the inheritance of the saints in light. He has delivered us from the power of darkness and conveyed us into the kingdom of the Son of his love in whom we have redemption through his blood, the forgiveness of sins.
>
> Colossians 1:12–15 (NKJV)

> For you did not receive a spirit that makes you a slave again to fear, but you received the Spirit of son-ship. And by him we cry, "Abba Father." The Spirit himself testifies with our spirit that we are God's children. Now if we are children, then we are heirs-heirs of God and co-heirs with Christ. If indeed we share in his sufferings in order that we may also share in his glory.
>
> Romans 8:15–17 (NIV)

Water Baptism

Our outward testimony of the inner change that happens to us when we believe in Jesus and commit ourselves to a life as his disciple is water baptism. This is the way we publicly announce our profession of faith in Jesus as our Savior. We need to obey the Word of God, which commands us to be baptized. Jesus, himself gave us a perfect example of obedience in water baptism in Matthew 3:13–16 (NIV).

> Then Jesus came from Galilee to the Jordan to be baptized by John (the Baptist). But John tried to deter him, saying, "I need to be baptized by you, and do you come to me?" Jesus replied, "Let it be so now; it is proper for us to do this to fulfill all righteousness. Then John consented. As soon as Jesus was baptized, he went up out of the water. At that moment heaven opened, and he saw the Spirit of God descending like a dove and lighting on him. And a voice from heaven said, "This is my Son, whom I love; with him I am well pleased."

To fully understand water baptism, we need to understand when we are born-again, the Spirit of God births us into the Body of Christ (the church). This spiritual baptism happens to every person who becomes a true Christian. It is done by God and is a spiritual transaction. We read about this in 1 Corinthians 12:12–13 (NIV).

The body is a unit, though it is made up of many parts; and through all its parts are many, they form one body. So it is with Christ. For we were all baptized by one Spirit into one body—whether Jews or Greeks, slave or free–and we were all given the one Spirit to drink.

> Or do you not realize that as many of us as were baptized in union with Christ Jesus were baptized in union with his death? So we are buried with him in death through baptism in order that, just as Christ rose from the dead through the Father's glorious power, so we too shall conduct ourselves in a new way of living. For if we have been united with him in a death like his; then the same must be true of our resurrection with him. Being aware of this that our old self was crucified with him, so that the power of a sin-controlled body might be done away with and we should no longer be slaves of sin, for a corpse is considered guiltless of sin. If then we have died with Christ, we believe that we shall also live with him, well assured that Christ, once risen from the dead, will not die anymore; death holds lordship over him no longer. The death he died was once for all to sin, but the life he lives, he lives to God. Similarly, let us consider

ourselves as actually dead to sin, but in Christ Jesus alive to God. Sin must not be king in your mortal body, to have you yield to its passions; neither must you offer the members of your body to serve sin as instruments of wickedness, but rather offer yourselves to God as living persons who rose from the dead, and present the members of your body to God as instruments of righteousness.

Romans 6:3–13 (ML)

Water baptism is the outward physical act that we participate in, in which we proclaim in outward testimony that this inward change has taken place in our life. This is a decision of our will. We must actively participate in doing it; just like Jesus did. It is our public statement to the world that we are dead to sin and alive in Christ. We do this by simple obedience to God's command.

This outward display of your inward change should be one of the first steps you take as you begin your new life as a disciple. As we read in the Bible about the first Christian believers, we find water baptism was obeyed quickly by those who came to Jesus. A classic example of this is in the eighth chapter of the book of Acts:

Then Philip opened his mouth, and began at the same scripture, and preached unto him Jesus. And as they went their way, they came unto a certain water: and the eunuch said, See, here is water; what doth hinder me to be baptized? And Philip said, If thou believest with all thine heart, thou mayest. And he answered and said, I believe that

Jesus Christ is the Son of God. And he commanded the chariot to stand still: and they went
down both into the water, both Philip and the
Eunuch; and he baptized him.

Acts 8:35–38 (KJV)

Another example of this is found in the book
of Acts. Peter had visited the home of Cornelius
and preached the gospel to them. Everyone present
believed and received the message. Notice what happened then:

While Peter was still speaking these words, the
Holy Spirit came on all who heard the message.
The circumcised believers who had come with
Peter were astonished that the gift of the Holy
Spirit had been poured out even on the Gentiles.
For they heard them speaking in tongues and
praising God. Then Peter said, "can anyone keep
these people from being baptized with water?
They have received the Holy Spirit just as we
have." So he ordered that they be baptized in the
name of Jesus Christ.

Acts 10:44–47 (NIV)

Immediately after believing by faith and accept-
ing the gospel message, Peter instructed them all to
be baptized in the name of Jesus Christ. The entire
household of Cornelius was happy to do so.

I pray that you too will not hesitate to be water
baptized once you have become a Christian so that
you can move forward with a good conscience before
God. If you believe with all your heart and have sin-

cerely repented of your sins, then there is no reason for you to be waiting. Obey the scriptures and be baptized in water in the name of Jesus Christ!

The Holy Spirit

As we learned in the first chapter, God the Father and Jesus, though differing in function, are *one*. We now need to learn of the third member, the Holy Spirit of God. The Scriptures clearly show the Father, Son, and Holy Spirit as *one*. The same as Jesus spoke of himself and the Father being one, he also spoke of himself and the Holy Spirit as being one. Let's look at some of the verses that show the Holy Spirit united with the Father and Son as the third member of the Trinity, dwelling among us.

> If you love me, you will obey what I command. And I will ask the Father, and he will give you another Counselor to be with you forever—The Spirit of Truth. The world cannot accept him, because it neither sees him nor knows him, But you know him, for he lives with you and will be in you. I will not leave you orphans; I will come to you ...
>
> John 14:16–18 NIV

Jesus replied, "If anyone loves me, he will obey my teaching, My Father will love him, and we will come to him and make our home with him ... "

John 14:23 NIV

And what agreement has the temple of God with idols? For you are the temple of the living God. As God has said: "I will dwell in them and walk among them. I will be their God, and they shall be my people." Therefore, "Come out from among them and be separate," says the Lord. "Do not touch what is unclean, and I will receive you. I will be a Father to you, and you shall be my sons and daughters, says the Lord Almighty."

2 Corinthians 6:16–18 (NKJV)

The Bible clearly teaches that the Father, Son, and Holy Spirit, at times may be seen separate in manifestation, yet never separate in being. The Holy Spirit can be understood as God among us. He dwells with us after we are born-again. We need to have the proper understanding of the Spirit so we can relate to him the right way. Our life should be walking daily in a living relationship with the Holy Spirit of God.

The Holy Spirit isn't some vague impression in our minds or a conviction in our hearts. He is God among us, and there are times he will speak to us. As we search the scripture, we find he has a mind, will, and emotions. We learn from the Bible that the Holy Spirit can be provoked, quenched, grieved, and even lied to. Let's look at some verses on this and then talk about it some more.

Now he who searches the hearts knows what the mind of the Spirit is, because he makes intercession for the saints according to the will of God.

Romans 8:27 (NKJV)

As they ministered to the Lord and fasted, the Holy Spirit said, "Now separate to me Barnabas and Saul for the work to which I have called them."

Acts 13:2 (NKJV)

After they had come to Mysia, they tried to go into Bithnia, but the Spirit did not permit them.

Acts 16:7 (NKJV)

And do not grieve the Holy Spirit of God, with whom you were sealed for the day of redemption.

Ephesians 4:30 (NIV)

Quench not the Spirit (KJV)
Do not stifle the Spirit (ML)
Do not smother the Spirit (LB)
Do not put out the Spirit's fire (NIV)

1 Thessalonians 5:19

Peter said, "Ananias, how is it that satan has so filled your heart that you have lied to the Holy Spirit ... " Peter said to her, "How could you agree to test the Spirit of the Lord?"

Acts 5:3–9 (NKJV)

A man who refused to obey the laws given by Moses was killed without mercy if there were two or three witnesses to his sin. Think how much more terrible the punishment will be for those who have trampled underfoot the Son of God and treated his cleansing blood as though it were common and unhallowed, and insulted and outraged the Holy Spirit who brings God's mercy to his people. For we know him who said, "Justice belongs to me; I will repay them," who also said, "The Lord himself will handle these cases." It is a fearful thing to fall into the hands of the living God.

Hebrews 10:28–31 (LB)

For us to walk in the fullness of the relationship God has for us, we need to believe without doubting the Holy Spirit is God among us. He is the living personal God who we can know and relate to in an intimate and real way. We should expect him to speak to us direction, personal correction, instruction, comfort, encouragement, and blessing.

This relationship will bring us into a Holy (set apart) lifestyle that includes our entire body, soul, and spirit.

Having therefore these promises, dearly beloved, let us cleanse ourselves from all filthiness of the flesh and spirit, perfecting holiness in the fear of God.

2 Corinthians 7:1 (KJV)

God commands us to possess our bodies in a clean and sin-free state.

Do you not know that your body is a temple of the Holy Spirit, who is in you, whom you have received from God? You are not your own; you were bought with a price. Therefore honor God with your body.

1 Corinthians 6:19–20 (NIV)

The Holy Spirit comes to our lives to change us in our soul from the old regenerate self to the new creation we are called to be. Moment by moment, we choose one decision at a time to yield to the Spirit and to become more like Jesus Christ.

Now understanding from the Word of God the Holy Spirit is a person (not human, but divine) who dwells among God's people, the same as Jesus once walked among the disciples; let's go on and find out more about him. We'll start in the Gospel of John where Jesus spoke about the Holy Spirit's coming.

But the Counselor, the Holy Spirit, who the Father will send in my name, will teach you all things and will remind you of everything I have said to you.

John 14:26 (NIV)

When the Counselor comes, whom I will send to you from the Father, the Spirit of Truth who goes out from the Father, he will testify about me.

John 15:26 (NIV)

But I tell you the truth: it is for your good that I am going away. Unless I am going away the Counselor will not come to you, but if I go, I will send him to you.

John 16:7 (NIV)

"I have much to say to you, more than you can now bear. But when the Spirit of Truth comes, he will guide you into all truth ... "

John 16:12–13 (NIV)

On several occasions Jesus spoke about and promised to send the Holy Spirit.

On one occasion, while he was eating with them (after his resurrection) he gave them this commandment: "Do not leave Jerusalem, but wait for the gift my Father promised, which you have heard me speak about. For John baptized with water, but in a few days you will be baptized with the Holy Spirit."

Acts 1:4 (NIV) (parenthesis added)

He said to them: "It is not for you to know the times or dates the Father has set by his own authority. But you will receive power when the Holy Spirit comes on you; and you will be my witnesses in Jerusalem, and in all Judea, and Samaria, and to the ends of the earth."

Acts 1:7–8 (NIV)

Now let's read of the actual coming of the Holy Spirit.

When the day of Pentecost came, they were all together in one place. Suddenly a sound like the blowing of a violent wind came from heaven and filled the whole house where they were sitting. They saw what seemed to be tongues of fire that separated and came to rest on each of them. All of

them were filled with the Holy Spirit and began to
speak in other tongues as the Spirit enabled them.

Acts 2:1–4 (NIV)

"In the last days, God says, I will pour out my
Spirit on all people. You sons and daughters will
prophecy, your young men will see visions, your
old men will dream dreams. Even on my servants,
both men and women, I will pour out my Spirit
in those days, and they will prophecy."

Acts 2:17–18 (NIV)

Peter replied, "Repent and be baptized, every one
of you in the name of Jesus Christ for the forgiveness of your sins, and you will receive the gift of
the Holy Spirit. The promise is for you and your
children and for all who are far off—for all whom
the Lord our God will call."

Acts 2:38–39 (NIV)

When the apostles in Jerusalem heard that
Samaria had accepted the Word of God, they
sent Peter and John to them. When they arrived,
they prayed for them that they might receive the
Holy Spirit, because the Holy Spirit had not yet
come upon any of them; they had simply been
baptized into the name of the Lord Jesus. Then
Peter and John placed their hands on them, and
they received the Holy Spirit.

Acts 8:14–17 (NIV)

Paul said, "John's baptism was a baptism of repentance. He told the people to believe the one coming after him, that is Jesus." On hearing this they
were baptized into the name of the Lord Jesus.

When Paul placed his hands on them the Holy
Spirit came on them, and they spoke in tongues
and prophesied. There were about twelve men in
all.

Acts 19:4–7, (NIV)

But be filled with the Spirit; Speaking to yourselves in psalms and hymns and spiritual songs,
singing and making melody in your heart to the
Lord.

Ephesians 5:18–19 (KJV)

Once the people believed and received the Holy
Spirit, they too became disciples of Jesus Christ
and began to proclaim the good news of the gospel. Wherever the disciples went preaching, miracles
happened, people were healed, and lives transformed.
People would receive Jesus as Savior and Lord, be
filled with the Holy Spirit, and begin to meet as the
church.

The work of the Holy Spirit in the life of a Chris-
tian is very real and powerful. If we want to receive
all God has for us, we need to be full of the Holy
Spirit. This is called by some as being "baptized in the
Holy Ghost." It is in receiving the Holy Spirit that
we come to be vessels that release the Spirit of God
and manifest the power and reality of Jesus Christ.
We become a pipeline for the delivery of the works of
God into our world. In 1 Corinthians, chapter twelve,
Paul writes about the gifts, which come from the
Holy Spirit and pass through our vessel. When we
have the Holy Spirit, we then have access to spiritual

gifts. The Bible clearly states that Jesus lives in the believer. Why then should we question whether his power will be seen in us? God expects us to be those who release the reality of Christ to the world around us by yielding to the manifestation of the gifts of the Holy Spirit! These gifts are the doorway to the reality of Jesus Christ being released. We should never see them as separate from the proclamation and manifestation of Jesus Christ in our midst. The gifts operate correctly when Jesus is Lord among us.

In the following verses, notice how it speaks to the manifestation of the gifts during a church service.

> But the manifestation of the Spirit is given to each one for the profit of all: for to one is given the word of wisdom through the Spirit, to another the word of knowledge through the same Spirit, to another faith by the same Spirit, to another gifts of healing by the same Spirit, to another the working of miracles, to another prophecy, to another discerning of spirits, to another different kinds of tongues, to another the interpretation of tongues. But the one and the same Spirit works all these things, distributing to each one individually as he wills.
>
> 1 Corinthians 12:7–11 (NKJV)

We need to be careful that we don't use this portion of scripture to limit the power and release of the Holy Spirit through our vessel. It is true that most of us will function in one or more of the gifts more readily than in the others; but when we are full of the Holy Spirit, we have the potential to be used in all the gifts. It is up to the Holy Spirit to grant these gifts as he wills (desires). When we are in the church, many of us will move in the gifts as the Spirit wills for that particular service. The Spirit may desire to use us in one gift in one service and a different gift in a different service. It is always good to remember:

> There are different kinds of gifts, but the same Spirit. There are different kinds of service, but the same Lord. There are different kinds of workings, but the same God works all of them in all men.
>
> 1 Corinthians 12:4–6 (NIV)

I hope you are beginning to realize our relationship with Jesus Christ involves the reality of God's power and presence through the Holy Spirit that can be clearly seen by the unbeliever. The Apostle Paul wrote: "For the kingdom of God is not in word, but in power" (1 Corinthians 4:20 KJV).

Before and beyond the release of the Holy Spirit's gifts through us, we should seek to know the government of Jesus Christ and his lordship over our personal lives. Our goal must never shift from abiding in the vine to producing the fruits and gifts. First and foremost, the presence of the Holy Spirit in our lives is to bring us to an ever-deeper relationship with Jesus Christ and his Word. As we abide in our place of relationship with him, we will then be free to release our faith and ask God to use us for his glory. Our perspective must always remain one of intimacy through submitted obedience. We do not just happen to stay there after we are born-again. We must deliberately seek to know Our Lord and learn to hear his voice (Holy Spirit) and leading. We have to live a life filled with passion for his presence, if we are to know the will of the Spirit and release his reality.

We shouldn't see our life as a Christian, as if someone walked up to the starting line and fired the pistol, expecting us to run the race of life out of our own intellect with the Bible as the written manual for us to check in on from time to time. Christianity isn't religion; it's a relationship! Knowledge of God without the reality of the Spirit's power and presence is simply man still eating from the Tree of the Knowledge of Good and Evil. We must cease from being led merely by our own intellect, deceived into believing that as long as we don't commit any known sin, we are all God wants us to be. Head knowledge of God, without a personal relationship with Christ that releases the Spirit's life in us and through us, is not God's intention. We need to live in the reality of the Spirit relationship. The normal life for us as a Christian should be a life of daily Bible study with the Spirit of God leading us in his plan and purpose.

> For as many as are led by the Spirit of God, these are the sons of God.
>
> Romans 8:14 (NKJV)

> If we live in the Spirit, let us walk in the Spirit.
>
> Galatians 5:25 (NKJV)

We must learn to live our lives in relationship with Christ, with our old man crucified and the new man being led of the Spirit, motivated by love. Our minds must be renewed to the serving of the Spirit's will and not our own. Christ's expectation of his church is that we, as members of his body, release his power and love to the world the same as he did. We accomplish this as we yield to the reality of God among us in the person of the Holy Spirit.

Spirit, Soul, and Body

In the same way that God can be seen as triune (three parts), so can we. Perhaps you have never thought of yourself as being a spirit man that possesses a soul and lives in a body. This is another truth we need to understand, if we are going to relate to God the way he wants us to.

Let's look at some verses which illustrate man is spirit, soul, and body (or what we call a triune or tripartite being):

> My soul magnifies the Lord, and my spirit has rejoiced in God my Savior ...
>
> Luke 1:46–47 (NKJV)

> Now may the God of peace himself sanctify you completely; and may your whole spirit, soul, and body be preserved blameless at the coming of our Lord Jesus Christ.
>
> 1 Thessalonians 5:23 (NKJV)

And do not fear those who kill the body but cannot kill the soul. But rather fear him who is able to destroy both soul and body in Hell

Matthew 10:28 (NKJV)

Now my soul is troubled, and what shall I say? "Father, save me from this hour? But for this purpose I came to this hour."

John 12:27 (NKJV)

And when Jesus cried out with a loud voice, he said, "Father into Your hands I commit My spirit."

Luke 23:46 (NKJV)

The spirit of man is the part created in the image of God and is born-again at the time of salvation. The Scripture is speaking of the spirit of man in II Corinthians, chapter five and verse seventeen, where we read; "Therefore, if anyone is in Christ he is a new creation; old things have passed away; behold all things have become new." When we receive Jesus, the perfect Spirit of God comes and lives in us. Our newborn spirit is now alive in Christ. The Spirit is now free to reveal or illuminate God to us. Until we are born-again and are alive spiritually we cannot even begin to understand the Bible!

The man without the Spirit does not accept the things that come from the Spirit of God, for they are foolishness to him, and he cannot understand them, because they are spiritually discerned.

1 Corinthians 2:14 (NIV)

Yet a time is coming and has now come when the
true worshipers will worship the Father in spirit
and in truth, for they are the kind of worshippers
the Father seeks. God is Spirit and his worshippers must worship in spirit and in truth.

John 4:23–24 (NIV)

It is through the spirit that we release prophecy,
tongues, healings, miracles, and other manifestations
of God's Spirit and power.

At the time of salvation, we are delivered from the
eternal penalty of death brought about by the sin of
Adam and our spirit is reborn. Christ comes to dwell
in our hearts by faith. The blood of Jesus washes us
clean from our sins and we stand before God in the
righteousness of Christ himself. The punishment we
deserved was placed on him at the cross and now
his righteousness is transferred or imputed to us.
We stand before God and he pronounces us justified
and forgiven before his eternal throne. Romans 5:1
(NIV) says, "Therefore, since we have been justified
through faith, we have peace with God through our
Lord Jesus Christ." Another way to explain this is; it
is just as if we had never sinned in the eyes of God.

Our soul is the part of us that thinks, reasons,
and moves in the realm of our intellect and emotions. Through the process of sanctification of the
soul, the Spirit of Christ that now dwells in us does a
work of renewal and change as we yield to the grace
and knowledge of Jesus Christ. Our sanctification
cannot be accomplished by our own struggling and

trying, but only by the Spirit as we yield ourselves to God and die to our old self. This is spoken of in 2 Corinthians 3:16–18 (NKJV):

> Nevertheless when one turns to the Lord, the veil is taken away. Now the Lord is the Spirit; and where the Spirit of the Lord is, there is liberty. But we all with unveiled face, beholding as in a mirror the glory of the Lord, are being transformed into the same image from glory to glory, just as by the Spirit of the Lord.

It is from our soul, as we yield to the Holy Spirit's influence, that we make decisions that produce either the fruits of the flesh or the fruits of the Spirit. At the time of our death here on earth; our soul will either go to heaven or to hell.

The body is our physical part, or the part of us we can see and touch. It is the temporal part of our being Paul called "our tent." It is born from the mother's womb, grows up, grows old, and dies. At the time of passing from this life we are delivered from the presence of sin.

> Now I say brethren, that flesh and blood cannot inherit the kingdom of God; nor does corruption inherit incorruption. Behold, I tell you a mystery; we shall not all sleep, but we shall all be changed - In a moment, in the twinkling of an eye, at the last trumpet. For the trumpet will sound, and the dead will be raised incorruptible, and we shall be changed. For this corruptible must put on incorruption, and this mortal must put on immortality.
> 1 Corinthians 15:50–53 (NKJV)

The Bible teaches us that our physical bodies will one day be resurrected (unless Jesus returns before we die) and then be glorified. All people who have lived physically, saved or unsaved, will one day be resurrected. Those of us who are saved will be resurrected/translated into eternal life (this is called glorification), while those who are not saved will be condemned to eternal damnation and hell.

It is important for you to be aware of these different aspects of your being and how they relate to Christ. You have been created spirit, soul, and body. Each of these areas are important to God and should be important to you as well.

By identifying these different parts of your personal make-up, we can rightly divide the scriptures as we read them. When we read of becoming new, we understand this is not talking about our body, but about our newborn spirit. When the Word talks of our changing and becoming more like Christ, we realize this is talking about the sanctification of the soul. When the Word tells us we will die we know it is talking of our body and not our soul. I give you these examples so as you are reading the Bible you will ask: what is the right way to divide this particular verse in applying it to myself?

A Mind to Change

Prior to receiving Jesus as Savior and Lord, our intellect operates within the realm of the fallen sin nature. Once we are born-again, our mind and will must be renewed to the revelation of God and his plan for us and for our lives. Our "old man" has moved in the realm of natural logic and reason. Our "new man" must be given to Christ as we begin to learn to walk by faith in the commands and revelation of God. We read in Isaiah 29:14 and again in 1 Corinthians 1:19 where God says, "I will destroy the wisdom of the wise; the intelligence of the intelligent I will frustrate" (NIV).

Let's go back to Genesis and see what God has revealed to us about the conflict between the person who has partaken of the knowledge of good and evil and the plan of God. As we read about Adam and Eve after their sin, they were dead in relation to the Spirit. They had no recourse other than to relate to life through the mind and intellect that was now controlled by their fallen sin nature. It was out of this fallen nature, or soul realm, that Adam and Eve discovered they were naked and needed covering. They then devised a plan out of their fallen nature to remedy this. It was both reasonable and logical for them to hide their nakedness by covering themselves with fig leaves, and so they did. This was contrary, however, to the plan of God. As we read on, we see God's divine way was through the death of an innocent animal and the shedding of blood, he would cover their nakedness. Man from this time onward has tried to cover his sin by works of his own. Out of the wisdom of man, Jesus becomes a stumbling block.

> See I lay a stone in Zion, a chosen and precious cornerstone, and the one who trusts in him will never be put to shame. Now to you who believe, this stone is precious. But to those who do not believe, the stone the builders rejected has become the capstone, and a stone that causes men to stumble and a rock that makes them fall. They stumble because they disobey the message
>
> 1 Peter 2:6–8 (NIV)

Man cannot relate to God out of the old nature that has not been renewed in Christ. This story of Adam and Eve's nakedness and their need of a covering speaks to us that our sins can never be covered by what we do, only by putting our trust in the shed blood of Jesus Christ.

This story also illustrates to us that we can never please God out of a mind that is not renewed and submitted to the plan of God. We begin to realize how God expects us to live a life, which is not led of our own concept of good and evil, and what we must do to approach him. We are not to be led of the mind, emotions, or logic, but rather by faith and by the Spirit. You and I can never please God with deeds that originate out of our flesh neither in getting saved nor in staying saved.

The will and purpose of God moves forward through our being led by the Spirit of God. The Spirit brings revelation to our spirit, which in turn illuminates our mind, and then we must submit ourselves to it. Any time we try to further the purpose of God, for ourselves or for the church through works originating out of our fallen nature instead of being led by the Spirit, we are creating dead works.

Once we are born-again, our mind needs to be renewed and submitted to the purpose of serving what God reveals to us as his will. Many times the will of God will be opposite of what our intellect will logically see as prudent. When this happens, we need to move forward, obediently walking by faith in God and not by sight. Without doing this, we can never please God. This is put in the right perspective by the verse in 2 Corinthians 5:7 (NIV), "We live by faith not by sight."

Being obedient to the leading of God will at times bring us to the end of ourselves, our own resources, and our abilities. This will require faith, which many times will not be the logical way for us to act. When our logic and reason disagree with the Word and the

Spirit, we must always be obedient and follow God. In order to do this, we need to learn to recognize what is the voice of God, the voice of the enemy, and our own intellectual self. It will be impossible for us to accomplish this unless we renew our minds to the will and plan of God by learning and knowing the scripture.

> Do not conform any longer to the pattern of this world, but be transformed by the renewing of your mind. Then you will be able to test and approve what God's will is—his good, pleasing and perfect will.
>
> Romans 12:2 (NIV)

> If indeed you have heard Him and have been taught by Him, as the truth is in Jesus: that you put off, concerning your former conduct, the old man which grows corrupt according to the deceitful lusts, and be renewed in the spirit of your mind, and that you put on the new man which was created according to God, in true righteousness and holiness.
>
> Ephesians 4:21–24 (NKJV)

This is part of the process we embrace when we say yes to Jesus. If we are to "take up our cross," we must deny our old carnal self and sinful desires and follow after our Lord. Jesus was referring to this in Romans chapter eight and verse six: "The mind of sinful man is death, but the mind controlled by the Spirit is life and peace" (NIV).

It is God's desire for us to grow and mature as a spirit man. As we grow and develop our life in the

Spirit and become more and more controlled by the new man, we become capable of receiving all he has for us. The scripture talks of this in Hebrews 5:14: "But solid food is for the mature who by constant use have trained themselves to distinguish between good and evil" (NIV).

Let me explain this some more. The only way we can come to live and walk in the Spirit is by simple obedience to God's Word, and being full of the Spirit. This is so important let me say it again. As a Christian, it is essential we be filled with the Spirit and covenant (join) with God to walk in submission to him and his Word.

This is difficult at first, because the spirit man within us is a baby, and the old carnal man is quite strong, since he has had his own way for so long. We have to be very careful to let the new spiritual nature be in control of our old carnal nature. This is going to take definite acts of our will to say yes to the still small voice of the Spirit, and no to the loud cry of our old man who is being crucified. If we obey without question, by faith the command of God, and deny without question all desire to be disobedient, we will begin to grow in being led of the Spirit. We must know in our hearts we can always obey.

> No temptation has seized you except what is common to man. And God is faithful; he will not let you be tempted beyond what you can bear. But when you are tempted, he will also provide a way out so that you can stand up under it.
>
> 1 Corinthians 10:13 (NIV)

The Scriptures teach us we have been given the ability to control our thoughts:

> We demolish arguments and every pretension that sets itself up against the knowledge of God, and we take captive every though to make it obedient to Christ
>
> 2 Corinthians 10:5 (NIV)

> Therefore gird up the loins of your mind, be sober, and rest your hope fully on the grace that is brought to you at the revelation of Jesus Christ;
>
> 1 Peter 1:13 (NKJV)

The battle for our footsteps will always be won or lost in the realm of the mind, as we exert our freewill to obey or disobey. As the Word and the Spirit are speaking to us "life" there will be the other voice, which will question God's leading. Examples such as, has God really said ...? Or isn't it more reasonable this way ...? Or, even if God is who he says he is, I don't think this would be like this! This other voice will come to argue on behalf of the way of death and disbelief. Until we can win this battle in our minds, we can never walk in the fullness of the Spirit and know the life of victory as a child of God. When we give in to the flesh, we soon find our hearing begins to go as we quench the Spirit. If we continue doing this, we soon fall back into a life of being controlled by our old self through the intellect, which operates from human logic instead of by faith.

Confusion follows the person who intellectually argues with the Spirit in the area of personal obedience. This can open the door to deception. Before long we will be worse off than we were before we were saved. It must be crystal clear to us that a *no* to God is a great big *yes* to the devil! If we attempt to intellectually decide which commands of God we are to obey and which to be philosophical about; we will find ourselves failing at everything God wants for us. We will feel more and more condemned, as we prove over and over again to ourselves and to everyone else that we can't ever be what God wants us to be. The end result of a person who intellectually argues with God is a person who lives beneath the purpose and privilege of their inheritance in Christ.

Many believers never cross this threshold from being controlled by their logic (self) and surrendering to being controlled by the Spirit. They simply never surrender in obedience to the Scripture and to being led of the Spirit past what they can understand and control. Because of their never relinquishing control (lordship) of their life to Jesus, they never experience the exciting new frontier of walking with the Holy Spirit in a life that is larger than they are.

Let us be those who refuse to settle for anything less than all God has for us in our relationship with him. There is an old saying that goes like this, "It's not for me to question why, it just for me to do or die." As we begin to walk in simple obedience, we release the Spirit of grace that makes us more and more into the image of Christ and leads us into a living relationship with God. In the Gospel of John, Jesus tells us:

"Whoever has my commands and obeys them, he is the one who loves me. he who loves me will be loved by my Father; and I too will love him and show myself to him ... If anyone loves me, he will obey my teaching, My Father will love him, and we will come to him and make our abode with him ... "

John 14:21–23 (NIV)

The man who says, "I know him," but does not do what he commands is a liar, and the truth is not in him. But if anyone obeys his word, God's love is truly made complete in him. This is how we know we are in him ...

1 John 2:4–5 (NIV)

I hope you are beginning to see how faith causes us to be obedient to God. As we walk in obedience, the Spirit of God abides with us and we find a liberty expressed as joy unspeakable and full of glory! How could it be anything else? For we now have fellowship with God! This fellowship isn't a mystical elusive thing, but rather a day by day walk of Bible fellowship; praying in the Spirit and being led by his voice.

Early on in our new life as a Christian, we need to realize it is not by might, nor by our effort, but by God's Spirit we now live. It is not our logic, but our faith that allows us to live a life where we seek God and his kingdom first, finding relationship with him as he adds all things to us, as we live, move, and have our being in Jesus Christ our Lord.

Will to Die

As his disciple, you will live a life of daily surrendering yourself completely to the lordship of Jesus. If you are wondering how much to surrender, I will tell you a story that illustrates this very well. As I remember, it went like this. There was a missionary ministering to a native group in Africa. Every night as the people gathered to hear the Word of God, they would bring gifts and lay them at the front of the church. Food, chickens, and other things of their poverty would be brought as offerings to the Lord. One night, as the missionary was speaking, a native fellow came forward with a large empty basket. After walking to the front and setting the basket down, he then got in it! For the remainder of the service, he continued sitting quietly in the basket. After the service was over, the missionary went to him and asked why he was sitting in the basket instead of sitting with the rest of the people in the chairs. The native fellow replied, "I am so poor I have nothing to give to my Jesus, so tonight I have made a decision to give him me!" You may find this particular demonstration of your surrendering to Christ a little radical or foreign to your way of thinking, but nonetheless, this needs to be in your heart if you are to follow Jesus. We need to quietly get down off the throne of our life and surrender it, all government, and all authority to God.

> So likewise, whosoever he be of you that forsaketh not all that he hath, he cannot be my disciple.
>
> Luke 14:33 (KJV)

> You are not your own, for you are bought at a price therefore glorify God in your body and your spirit, which are God's
>
> 1 Corinthians 6:20 (NKJV)

> Thou art worthy, O Lord, to receive glory and honor and power: for thou hast created all things, and for thy pleasure they are and were created.
>
> Revelation 4:11 (KJV)

> Not that I have already obtained all this, or have already been made perfect, but I press on to take hold of that for which Christ Jesus took hold of me. Brothers, I do not consider myself yet to have taken hold of it. But one thing I do: Forgetting what is behind and straining toward what is ahead, I press on toward the goal to win the prize for which God has called me heavenward in Christ Jesus.
>
> Philippians 3:12–14 (NIV)

I want to make sure you do not fall into the error of many, by believing your act of repentance at the time of receiving Jesus qualifies you as being a Christian disciple. Have you given up ownership of yourself yet? The initial act of surrender to Jesus must become a lifestyle of yielding to his will. As disciples, we must live in the land of change as Christ molds us into his image. The Holy Spirit day by day, as we allow him, shows us areas of our life we need to correct. When he shows us an area that doesn't conform to the Word we simply need to repent of our way and conform to his.

This attitude toward our Christian walk is not something we simply mature into. We must never leave our place of surrender. This means we can't postpone repentance, obedience, or yielding to the Spirit. There will never be a better time when it is easier, or more convenient to do these things than right now. When we decide to wait, hoping it will be easier later, we are simply deceiving ourselves and quenching the Spirit. Do it now!

There is an initial critical decision that needs to be made in regard to our following Christ or continuing with some former friendships and lifestyles.

> Of course, your former friends will be very surprised when you don't eagerly join them anymore in the wicked things they do, and they will laugh at you in contempt and scorn.
>
> 1 Peter 4:4 (LB)

Do not be misled: "Bad company corrupts good character."

1 Corinthians 15:33 (NIV)

You adulterous people, don't you know that friendship with the world is hatred toward God! Anyone who chooses to be a friend of the world becomes an enemy of God.

James 4:4 (NIV)

Jesus Christ isn't something you add to your life, he is the Lord who brings repentance to the old way and opens the door to the new. A night alone at home with God is worth a thousand nights out with friends and sin. He was willing to die for you. Are you willing to give up your former worldly lifestyle and surrender to him?

Any sin can be simply repented of, and we can live the rest of our lives free from it. If this wasn't true, then Christ died in vain. We need to believe in the power of his blood and the change it seeks to produce in us. We should never let anyone tell us we have a sin in our life that is the kind we can't leave behind out of simple repentance and by our willful choice to deny it. When we humble ourselves in confession and repentance, followed by a sincere desire and prayer to God to be free from our sin, he is more than able to set us free.

Prior to my conversion, I was a terribly sinful man, and many have wondered at my deliverance from sin. I don't believe I would have ever been able to break free if I hadn't been shown a verse in James

5:16, where it tells us to confess our faults (sins) to each other, and pray for each other. I found if I had a sin in my life I couldn't be free of, I would vow to myself if I did it again, I would confess it to the body and ask them to pray with me for deliverance. When I would go confess my sin and the people would lay hands on me and intercede on my behalf, I would be delivered. This was a very painful thing and humbled me more than I thought it would; but in the end, I can say every time I have dealt with my sin in this way, God has totally delivered me. As we live with a cry in our hearts to be free from sin, the Holy Spirit is faithful to deliver us. The blood of Christ has broken the power of sin in our lives as Christians. I believe you too will walk with this fervent desire to be free from sin as you seek to live for him.

We must never lose the cry within our hearts that says, "God, I am willing to change. I will obey you no matter the costs. From this time forward, when the Word of God says the opposite of what my mind and my fleshly desires say, I will obey your Word." We must decide, no matter how good the devil and our mind makes it seem, if it is outside of God, it is off limits to us. Until we realize we must say no to the devil, and crucify our own desires and self-will, we will not follow God into the realm of the Spirit.

There are two natures within us in conflict, the old carnal man and the new man in Christ. This will continue to be so until the time of our physical death here on earth. The Spirit of God will be influencing us to respond to him out of our renewed mind, while the devil will be appealing to our natural minds to give in to our old nature and go with him. But it is we who stand and cast the deciding vote. When we choose the right way, we produce the fruits of the Spirit and the life of Jesus is released. When we choose wrong, we quench this life and produce the fruits of the flesh, which is sin.

> The acts of the sinful nature are obvious: sexual immorality, impurity and debauchery; idolatry and witchcraft; hatred, discord, jealousy, fits of rage, selfish ambition, dissensions, factions, and envy; drunkenness, orgies and the like. I warn you, as I did before, that those who live like this will not inherit the kingdom of God. But the fruit of the Spirit is love, joy, peace, patience, kindness, goodness, faithfulness, gentleness and self-control. Against such things there is no law. Those who belong to Christ Jesus have crucified the sinful nature with its passions and desires. Since we live by the Spirit, let us keep in step with the Spirit.
>
> Galatians 5:19–25 (NIV)

> Since then, you have been raised with Christ, set your heart on things above, where Christ is seated at the right hand of God. Set your affections on things above, not on earthly things. For you died, and your life is now hidden with Christ in God. When Christ who is your life, appears, then you also will appear with him in glory.
>
> Colossians 3:4 (NIV)

This conflict between the old man desiring sin, and the new man obeying God will be lost by us, if we don't pursue the renewing of our minds as we are told to in the Word. As we wash ourselves daily in the Word, prayer, worship, and praise, our spirit man is fed and changes are worked in us through the sanctification of our souls. We decide this battle every day by the life we live and the thoughts we think and the choices we make.

> Finally brothers, whatever is true, whatever is noble, whatever is right, whatever is pure, whatever is lovely, whatever is admirable—if anything is excellent or praiseworthy—think about such things.
>
> Philippians 4:8 (NIV)

This reminds me of a story I once heard from a pastor that I think you'll appreciate. There was a terrible character in Alaska during the time of the gold rush. He would come into a town with two dogs. One was a big white Malamute, the other was an ugly little black mutt. The man would hang around the town for a day or two and solicit bets on which dog could whip the other one. Just about everybody would bet on the large white dog. It was clear the Malamute was larger and stronger and the black mutt would be no match for this magnificent creature. After the man would get all the bets placed, he would put the two dogs together and the little black dog would whip the daylights out of the white one. One day he revealed how this worked, saying it was quite simple. Since arriving in town, he simply fed the black dog and starved the white one! By the time the dogs had to fight, the white dog was so weak he couldn't defend himself.

This is a clear example of our daily walk as a disciple. The darkness we came out of is no match for the glorious light we've been born into. All we have to do is feed our white dog (the new spirit man) and starve our black one (the old carnal man). We must learn to live our lives in such a way as to get up every morning, chain the black dog without food, and feed and water the white dog. This process of sanctification is accomplished in us daily as we live a life of unconditional surrender to Christ and allow the Holy Spirit to produce his fruits as we say yes to his divine influence. Let's look at some verses on this.

> So I say, live by the Spirit, and you will not gratify the desires of the sinful nature. For the sinful nature desires what is contrary to the Spirit, and the Spirit what is contrary to the sinful nature; they are in conflict with each other.
> Galatians 5:16 (NIV)

> Those who belong to Christ Jesus have crucified the sinful nature with its passions and desires.
> Galatians 5:24 (NIV)

> The one who sows to please his sinful nature, from that nature will reap destruction; the one who sows to please the Spirit, from the Spirit will reap eternal life.
> Galatians 6:8 (NIV)

Love

The Bible sometimes uses single words to describe God. We find one of these in 1 John 4:16 (KJV) where it simply says, "God is love."

Now this can bring us to a dilemma; if we interpret love by what we see around us in the world, it could make us sick to our stomach! We quickly realize what the world thinks is love is simply man seeking gratification and experience at the expense of others. Movie stars stir the hearts and emotions of the masses. Their broken and corrupt personal lives, however, often reflect a false reality. They themselves only dream of the love they so gallantly act out on screen. So how can we know or identify love?

One thing that helped me understand love was when I learned the word love was actually three words in the Greek language spoken during the time of Christ. They used the word *eros* to signify sexual (fleshly) love; the word *phileo* to signify emotional (of the soul) love; and *agape* to signify selfless (spiritual) love.

Many people get themselves into great difficulties being led of the flesh, believing that sexual love alone will bring lasting happiness. It will not! Then another difficulty can arise when our love is founded on emotion. Have you ever noticed how some couples can be so in love one minute and then hate each other the next? That's because their relationship is based on emotional love. If we want to have an enduring and stable love, then we must also have the selfless, or Spirit, love.

It is the Spirit or "agape" love we see in Jesus's death on the cross; while we were still sinners, and living outside his kingdom; he loved us enough to die for us.

> But God demonstrates his own love for us in this: while we were still sinners, Christ died for us.
>
> Romans 5:8 (NIV)

> Greater love has no man than this that he lay down his life for his friends
>
> John 15:13 (NIV)

As Jesus' disciples, we are to show this same selfless, agape love to those around us.

> A new commandment I give you: love one another. As I have loved you, so you must love one another. By this all men will know that you are my disciples, if you love one another.
>
> John 13:34–35 (NIV)

Be imitators of God, therefore, as dearly loved children live a life of love, just as Christ loved us and gave himself up for us as a fragrant offering and sacrifice to God.

Ephesians 5:1 (NIV)

Now that you have purified yourselves by obeying the truth so that you have sincere love for your brothers, love one another deeply from the heart,

1 Peter 1:22 (NIV)

Jesus tells us it is by our selfless agape love that others will know we are his disciples. This agape love is to extend to our enemies and to those who hate us and mistreat us.

You have heard that it is said Love your neighbor and hate your enemy. But I tell you: love your enemies and pray for those who persecute you, that you may be sons of your Father in heaven.

Matthew 5:43–45 (NIV)

As the Lord's disciples, we do not have the luxury of picking and choosing who we love or don't love.

He who says he is in the light and hates his brother is in the darkness still. He who loves his brother abides in the light, and in it there is no cause for stumbling.

1 John 2:9–11 (RS)

And when you stand praying, forgive, if ye have anything against any, that your Father also, who is in heaven, may forgive you your trespasses. But if

you do not forgive, neither will your Father, who
is in heaven, forgive your trespasses.

Mark 11:25–26 (NKJ)

Let's look at what the Bible says are the attri-
butes of love:

Love is patient, love is kind. It does not envy, it
does not boast, it is not proud. It is not rude, it is
not self-seeking, it is not easily angered, it keeps
no records of wrongs. Love does not delight in
evil but rejoices with the truth. It always protects,
always trusts, always hopes, always preservers.
Love never fails.

1 Corinthians 13:4–8 (NIV)

These are the qualities of love, with which God
relates to us; and these are the qualities we are to
express as we relate to God and others.

As a young boy, there were times when my
mother would call to me to get up and go to school
and I would respond with, "I'm sick." This was never
taken as true, simply on the basis of one young boy's
feelings and beliefs, but instead was investigated by
my mother. She would always go to the cupboard
and get the thermometer. She would then come
to my bedside and measure my temperature. If the
thermometer proved I had a fever and was truly sick,
she would allow me to stay home for the day and get
well. But if I did not have a fever, she would insist
that even though I felt sick and wanted to be sick for
the day, I simply wasn't sick. I would then get up and
go to school.

The same way my mother measured my illness—not by my feelings, but by my temperature—so has Jesus given us a way to measure our love for him: "If you love me you will obey what I command," (John 14:15 NIV). As we see from this scripture, our love for the Lord is measured by our obedience to him.

When asked of all the commandments, which was the most important, Jesus answered:

> "The most important one," answered Jesus, "is this: 'Hear O Israel, the Lord our God, the Lord is one. Love the Lord your God with all your heart and with all your soul and with all your mind and with all your strength.' The second is this: 'Love your neighbor as yourself.' There is no commandment greater than these."
>
> Mark 12:29–31 (NIV)

The selfless relationship of love that God offers us through Jesus Christ should inspire us to no longer be self-centered, but instead to become God centered. When this happens we begin to look for ways to love and serve God and others. The Apostle John encourages us:

> Dear friends, let us love one another, for love comes from God. Everyone who loves has been born of God and knows God. Whoever does not love does not know God, because God is love. This is how God showed his love among us: He sent his one and only Son into the world that we might live through him. This is love: not that we loved God, but that he loved us and sent his Son

as an atoning sacrifice for our sins. Dear friends, since God loved us, we also ought to love one another. No one has ever seen God, but if we love one another, God lives in us and his love is made complete in us.

1 John 4:7–12 (NIV)

Love is a very practical thing in our daily lives:

"'For I was hungry and you gave me something to eat, I was thirsty and you gave me something to drink. I was a stranger and you invited me in, I needed clothes and you clothed me, I was sick and you looked after me, I was in prison and you came to visit me.' Then the righteous will answer him, 'Lord when did we see you hungry and feed you, or thirsty and give you something to drink? When did we see you a stranger and invite you in, or needing clothes and clothe you?' Then the King will reply, 'I tell you the truth, whatever you did for one of the least of these brothers of mine, you did to me.'"

Matthew 25:35–40 (NIV)

Religion that God our Father accepts as pure and faultless is this: to look after orphans and widows in their distress and to keep oneself from being polluted by the world

James 1:27 (NIV)

And I pray that you, being rooted and established in love, may have power, together with all the saints, to grasp how wide and long and high and deep is the love of Christ, and to know this love that passes knowledge—that you may be filled to the measure of all the fullness of God. Now to him who is able to do immeasurably more than all we ask or imagine, according to his power that is at work within us, to him be glory in the church and in Christ Jesus throughout all generations, for ever and ever Amen.

Ephesians 3:17–20 (NIV)

I pray most fervently that you understand that we must develop our lives as disciples in love. This is a love of God, which inspires us to be like him. This is a love that comes through us from Jesus himself.

You Must Eat

My friend, when you were a newborn child, you weren't able to walk yet. Your head was large, your body small, and your legs were just too little to support you. As a newborn Christian, that's how you are spiritually. You're a babe in Christ. The life in you is real life, and it is perfect (of God's Spirit); but you still need to grow in grace and knowledge. You have received life in your spirit, but now just like a newborn child, you need to eat in order to grow and become a mature man or woman of God. So how do we eat? You eat by reading the Word of God.

You must learn the footsteps of relationship with God, which he has laid out in his Word. Blessings will come to us as we live in unity with him. Simply put, to walk with God, we must know his Word and we must become obedient to the life it shows us we are to live in him. Feeding on the Word of God is "step number one" for every new believer. We find in 1 Peter 2:1–2 (NKJV).

> Therefore, laying aside all malice, all deceit, envy,
> and all evil speaking, as newborn babes, desire the
> pure milk of the word, that you may grow thereby.

Of our own freewill, we choose a life of reading and studying the Scriptures and of conforming ourselves to them, thus becoming a disciple of Jesus. If we choose not to, and continue on as masters of our own lives, we will never know Jesus like we should. As a disciple of Christ, we need to commit our lives to the Word. Without doing so, it will not matter which church we go to, how much we pray, or the amount of money we give. We will never mature as God desires unless we commit ourselves to the daily reading of the Word and accept it as the perfect revelation of God to man.

God promises special blessings to those who will study and reverence his Word. He promised Joshua if he would meditate upon the Word day and night, not letting the "Word of the Law" depart from his mouth, being careful to do all it commanded him to do, he would make his way prosperous, and he would have good success (Joshua 1:8). We also read in Psalms that when our delight is in the law of the Lord, and we meditate on it day and night, we will be like a tree planted by the rivers of water. We will bring forth fruit in due season and our leaves will not wither, and whatever we do will prosper (Read Psalms 1:1–3).

We read the Word of God in faith believing, we too will receive these blessings. I am reminded of a little song I learned long ago that goes like this:

Every promises in that blessed book is mine
Every chapter, every verse, and every line
And I know God's Word is true
It applies to me and you
Every promise in that Blessed Book is mine
(author unknown)

We need to know in our hearts that Scripture is fact; it is inspired by God, and it is the roadmap we build our lives on. Let me give you some scripture to back this up:

It is written man shall not live by bread alone, but by every word of God

Luke 4:4 (NKJV)

Heaven and earth will pass away, but my words will never pass away.

Mark 13:31 (NIV)

I will worship toward Your holy temple, and praise Your name for Your loving kindness and Your truth; For You have magnified Your word above all your name.

Psalms 138:2 (NKJV)

All Scripture is God breathed and is useful for teaching, rebuking, correcting and training in righteousness, so the man of God may be thoroughly equipped for every good work.

II Timothy 3:16–17 (NIV)

The Word of God is living, and powerful, and sharper than any two-edged sword, piercing even to the division of soul and spirit, and of joints and marrow, and is a discerner of the thoughts and intents of the heart.

Hebrews 4:12 (NKJV)

How can a young man cleanse his way? By taking heed according to your word ... Your word is a lamp to my feet and a light to my path.

Psalms 119:9–105 (NKJV)

I saw heaven standing open and there before me was a white horse, whose rider is called Faithful and True. With justice he judges and makes war. His eyes are like blazing fire, and on his head are many crowns. He has a name written on him that no one knows but he himself. He is dressed in a robe dipped in blood, and his name is the Word of God. The armies of heaven were following him ...

Revelation 19:11–14 (NIV)

The Bible, though recorded on paper by men, was authored by God as the Holy Spirit moved upon man. It is God revealed to us today. Is this the only way God reveals himself? No! But any true revelation of God will always be in perfect agreement with the written Word. Notice how the Apostle Peter spoke of the supremacy of the written Word:

For he (Jesus) received honor and glory from God the Father when the voice came to him from the majestic glory saying, "This is my Son, whom I love; with him I am well pleased." We ourselves heard this voice that came from heaven when we were with him on the sacred mountain. And we have the word of the prophets made more certain, and you will do well to pay attention to it, as to a light shining in a dark place, until the day dawns and the morning star rises in your hearts. Above all, you must understand that no prophecy of Scripture came about by the prophet's own intention. For prophecy never had its origin in the will of man, but men spoke from God as they were carried along by the Holy Spirit.

II Peter 1:17–21 (NIV) (parenthesis added)

The origin of the Bible is not simply in the will of man. The Scriptures are not just fanciful words or mere opinions of religious men. My Christian friend, let no one mislead you on this point! The Bible is literally inspired and authored by God himself. As we read in the following verse, we will do well to pay attention to it. "Study to show thyself approved unto God, a workman that needeth not to be ashamed, rightly dividing the word of truth" (II Timothy 2:15 KJV). Notice what the following scripture says in reference to Christ and his care of the church.

That he might sanctify and cleanse her with the washing of water by the word, that he might present her to himself a glorious church, not having spot or wrinkle or any such thing, but that she should be holy and without blemish.

Ephesians 5:26 (NKJV)

How is the church made holy and spotless without even a blemish or wrinkle? It is by the washing of water by the Word! As we read the Word, we are cleansed and made new.

The consistent ministry of the Word must be the foundation of every disciple. Hearing the teaching and preaching of the Word and personally studying it on our own, is a sweeping, cleansing work that must be a part of our daily lives. If we will regularly study the Bible and listen to it being taught and preached by anointed ministers; we will have the foundation necessary that will enable us to grow up into a strong and healthy man or woman of God. We will be fit for every good work.

If we will not embrace the Word, and read it regularly, we will become out of balance and weak. Before long, we will end up in the wilderness, where the enemy will be feeding us only small portions of scripture, which he will take out of context, distort, and we will wrongfully apply. When this happens, we never mature and miss the will of God for our lives.

There is no true discipleship outside of a lifestyle submitted to the written Word. A person needs to begin to read the Bible and grow after being born-again. If you don't, you will find yourself returning to the life you were living before, just as if nothing had ever happened. You might go and join a church somewhere and begin to base your discipleship on what others are doing and saying around you. We are warned of this in 2 Corinthians 10:12 (KJV).

We dare not make ourselves of the number, or compare ourselves with some that commend themselves: but they measuring themselves by themselves and comparing themselves among themselves, are not wise.

To illustrate this in a different way, let me tell you about when I was a young man working on a cattle ranch. While I was there, I befriended another young man who was only seventeen at the time. He was quite a cowboy, and was very talented in riding the horses and bulls. Every weekend he would go to a local rodeo competition and win money. One day, he said he had applied for his professional card so he could compete with the world champions. I asked my friend why he would want to do this when he was winning money all the time where he was. I have never forgotten what he said to me: "I'm afraid if I don't go compete with the professionals, I will soon become just like all the other amateurs and never amount to anything." Throughout the years, that young man went on to win some of the biggest rodeos in the world, while most of the amateurs he once rode against settled into mediocrity. This is what will happen to us spiritually, if we don't get into the Scripture early in our life with God. We need to start reading about the mighty men and women of God and begin to live like them in the arena of faith!

We must feed ourselves out of the Word if we want to become a David, a Deborah, a Peter, or a Paul. As we study the Word with a pure heart, the Holy Spirit builds our spirit, which in turn works in our souls to produce change. We find ourselves being filled with faith and a new perspective of who we are in Christ and what he wants for our lives.

To yield to Christ means to submit our lives in agreement to the written Word. The more we understand who God is, the more we will know who we are in him. A simple way to say this is, "The only way to know who you are is to know who your God is." And the way to know who God is, is by reading and studying the Bible.

Rest

There is a basic difference between Christianity and all other religions of the world. Other religions exist on what man must do for God, while Christianity rests on what God has done for man. While they all say "do," the cross of Christ says "done"! In other religions, we must earn our standing before God. In Christianity, we receive our standing through believing in what has been done by Christ's blood sacrifice. Only by faith in the unmerited gift of salvation, through the death of Jesus Christ, can we ever be right in our relationship with God.

Christians rest in knowing they are redeemed and now are at peace with God. Those of other religions live never sure of their place in this life, nor the one to come. While they strive and work to obtain their place before God, the Christian rests in faith knowing they have already obtained it.

The Word tells us the only righteousness God

is ever going to accept from a human being is the righteousness he places on us (imputes) when we put our complete faith in the sacrifice of Jesus Christ. It is through the act of repentance of our sins, and our belief in the shedding of Christ's blood we are cleansed from sin and are saved. It is through our belief that we are redeemed from our fallen state and reconciled to God. The blood of Jesus cleanses us from our sins and restores us to fellowship with God, placing us into the same perfect righteous state of Christ himself.

One night I was travailing in prayer and trying my best to get a cool drop of water for my circumstances. I felt the Spirit say to me, "If Billy Graham was on one side of you and Oral Roberts on the other, and they were praying like you, I wouldn't hear it! You must quit trying to relate to me out of who you are and begin to approach me out of faith in who I am and what I've done."

Until we can rest without trying to improve on the completed work of Christ, we will never experience the full release of God's grace into our lives the way we should. As we walk with God, we must be careful to never stray from the faith we have in the transferred righteousness of Christ. From the time we are saved forward, we should never leave our place of rest in knowing all our righteousness comes from Jesus. It is our faith in him that releases the divine influence of God's Spirit (grace) to live through us and change us from glory to glory. When we lose sight of this, we begin to try and establish our own righteousness by our own works (effort).

An example of our walk of grace is seen in the Old Testament where God commanded the priests to not wear anything that caused sweat if they were going to minister to him. This is an example of how we shouldn't let self-effort enter into our walk of grace. As we walk in the Spirit, we must never lose our rest of faith in the finished work of Christ and his blood.

Once we are at rest, we need to keep feeding on the Word and listening to the still small voice of the Spirit within us as we live in our relationship of faith and fellowship with our Lord. We must be careful that we don't fall back into a life dominated by the flesh. This will quench the Spirit to the point we no longer hear him, and our fallen nature will have regained control. We can actually neglect our relationship with him until we no longer know his presence. It's easy to let this happen and then say, "I'm resting in grace," when what we have really done is become so cold we are no longer in fellowship with him. We must live at rest in our place of complete forgiveness and acceptance before the throne of God! This must not become an excuse though for not living in relationship with him. We should not allow ourselves to fall into a religious routine living beneath the Spirit realm dominated by our carnal mind instead of our communion with the Spirit with our minds renewed. The need to press into God while at the same time resting in our perfect standing before him is one of the biggest challenges we face in our Christians walk.

Never allow the devil to lead you to believe there is something wrong between you and God. When we sin, the Holy Spirit will bring conviction to us. If and when this happens, we must repent as soon as possible for our sins, but never doubt the reality of your new birth. The enemy is forever trying to get us to fail in the realm of the soul (flesh) and then convince us the perfect work of the new spirit man isn't real. Some people find it necessary to write the exact date, year, and place of their born-again experience in their Bible. Never doubt your salvation! If you buy into this, you lose your peace and begin to try to do what has already been done at the cross! When we live in this deception and torment of self-condemnation, we actually deny Christ by turning away from his grace and try to substitute it with works of our own. When this happens, we cease to walk in the Spirit by faith and begin to slip into what is called legalism. When we discover ourselves trying to relate to God out of our works or lack of works we need to ask forgiveness. This will release God's grace so it can flow freely again through us to produce his life and fruit.

One of the biggest reasons why so many of us have trouble with this is because we have never settled the issue of how God the Father feels about us. For too long, Satan has confused us by doing evil and then blaming God, while at the same time trying to take credit for all the good God has done.

For this reason, most of us need to be corrected in our understanding of God's attitude toward us. We have a vague impression that he is sometimes happy, sometimes mad, and usually a little grouchy. Many of us go years feeling that he may be happy with everyone else, but surely not with us. We are so vain at times that we actually think God carries a little grudge against us personally. Satan is forever trying to deceive us into believing God isn't love. He wants us to live in condemnation instead of abiding in the truth we are loved and received by God.

> How great is the love the Father has lavished on us, that we should be called children of God! And that is what we are!
>
> 1 John 3:1 (NIV)

> Now therefore, you are no longer strangers and foreigners, but fellow citizens with the saints and members of the household of God.
>
> Ephesians 2:19 (NIV)

We are tempted to see our coming to Christ as a door opening a crack so we can peek through and see God. We then begin struggling to find acceptance before this far off God who will, on rare occasions, be mindful of us. This is so wrong! The scriptures so clearly show us we have been adopted into the household. We are joint heirs with Christ. When we are born-again, we must understand we have walked up to the door of God and it has swung wide open to us. The God of eternity has declared us accepted and he is pleased with us. Our relationship is an established fact in God's heart. We are now seated at the family table of God, partaking of his unlimited blessings. Release your faith and unlock the life God has for you!

> What then shall we say to these things? If God is for us, who can be against us? He who did not spare his own Son, but delivered him up for us all, how shall he not with him freely give us all things?
>
> Romans 8:31–32 (NKJV)

Let's go back to Genesis and move forward as we look at the heart of our Heavenly Father toward us. Before we do, let's read these verses that will help:

> Then Peter opened his mouth and said: "In truth I perceive that God shows no partiality. But in every nation whoever fears him, and works righteousness is accepted by him."
>
> Acts 10:34–35 (NKJV)

> For as many of you as were baptized into Christ have put on Christ. There is neither Jew nor Greek, there is neither male nor female; for you are all one in Christ Jesus.
>
> Galatians 3:27–28 (NKJV)

Now let us agree to believe and accept these verses as applying to us. We are no special exception in the plan of salvation. If you have received Jesus as Lord and have forsaken your sin; then if God has ever loved anyone and accepted them, he loves and accepts you! If we see ourselves different than this; we simply do not have complete and accurate faith in Jesus Christ.

Remember the account of the Garden of Eden where we said there were two kinds of trees mentioned by name? We have already talked about the Tree of the Knowledge of Good and Evil, but what about the other tree? It was the Tree of Life. God said they could eat of all the trees except the Tree of the Knowledge of Good and Evil. The Tree of Life was there for man to partake of. In the garden, God gave man the choice of eternal life with him or the choice to disobey and die. If Adam and Eve had not disobeyed God, they could have eaten of the Tree of Life and stayed in the garden. There would have been no fall of man, nor would death have come to the human race. God's intention for man is still the same; he provides the way of life, and man must choose to partake of life or refuse and die.

Now that we see this let's move forward and follow the heart of God toward us as he seeks to bless and save his children:

> Then God blessed them, and God said to them, be fruitful and multiply; fill the earth and subdue it.
> Genesis 1:28 (NKJV) (spoken to Adam and Eve)

> So God blessed Noah and his sons, and said to them: be fruitful and multiply, and fill the earth.
> Genesis 9:1 (NKJV)

> I will surely bless you and make your descendants as numerous as the stars of the sky and the sand on the seashore.
> Genesis 12:2 (NKJV) (spoken to Abraham)

And Abram was very rich in cattle, in silver, and in gold.

Genesis 13:2 (KJV)

I will bless you and make your descendants as numerous as the stars of the sky and as the sand on the seashore.

Genesis 22:17 (NKJV)

Isaac planted crops in that land and the same year reaped a hundred-fold because the Lord blessed him. The man became rich, and his wealth continued to grow until he became wealthy... That the night the LORD appeared to him and said, "I am the God of your Father Abraham. Do not be afraid, for I am with you; I will bless you and will increase the number of your descendants for the sake of my servant Abraham."

Genesis 26:12–13, 24 (NIV)

The LORD said to Moses, "Tell Aaron and his sons, 'this is how you are to bless the Israelites. Say to them: the LORD bless you and keep you; the Lord make his face to shine upon you and be gracious to you; the Lord turn his face toward you and give you peace.' So they will put my name on the Israelites, and I will bless them."

Numbers 6:22–27 (NIV)

I have received commandment to bless; and he (God) has blessed, and I cannot change it.

Numbers 23:20 (NIV)

If you fully obey the LORD your God and carefully follow all his commands I give you today, the LORD your God will set you on high above all the nations on earth. All these blessings will come upon you and accompany you if you obey the LORD your God. You will be blessed in the city and blessed in the country. The fruit of your womb will be blessed and the crops of your land and the young of your livestock—the calves of your herds and the lambs of your flocks. Your basket and your kneading trough will be blessed. You will be blessed when you come in and blessed when you go out. The LORD will grant that the enemies who rise up against you will be defeated before you. They will come at you from one direction but flee from you in seven. The LORD will send a blessing on your barns and on everything you put your hand to. The LORD your God will bless you in the land he is giving you. The LORD will establish you as his holy people, as he promised you on oath, if you keep the commands of the LORD your God and walk in his ways. Then all the people of the earth will see that you are called by the name of the LORD, and they will fear you. The LORD will grant you abundant prosperity—in the fruit of your womb, the young of your livestock and the crops of your ground—in the land he swore to your forefathers to give you. The LORD will open the heavens, the storehouse of his bounty, to send rain on your lands. You will lend to many nations but will borrow from none. The Lord will make you the head, not the tail. If you pay attention to the commands of the LORD your

God that I give you this day and carefully follow them, you will always be at the top, never at the bottom.

Deuteronomy 28:1–13 (NIV)

Now let's look at some verses that show us all the blessings God promised to Abraham and the nation of Israel are now ours through Jesus Christ!

Christ redeemed us from the curse of the law by becoming a curse for us, for it is written: "Cursed is everyone who is hung on a tree." He redeemed us in order that the blessings given to Abraham might come to the Gentiles (us) through Christ Jesus, so that by faith we might receive the promise of the Spirit.

Galatians 3:13&14 (NIV) (parenthesis added)

And if you are Christ's, then you are Abraham's seed, and heirs according to the promise.

Galatians 3:29 (NKJV)

In resting in the finished work of Christ's blood, which has paid the penalty for our sins and reconciled us to God, we also find we have been adopted into the family of Israel and have become sons and daughters of Abraham, the father of our faith. This seals us into God's covenant which he made with Abraham and extends to us. Let us read how that is the anchor to our knowing God loves us and has covenanted/promised to bless us here in this life as well as forever.

For when God made promise to Abraham, because he could swear by no greater, he swore by himself, Saying, "Surely blessing I will bless you, and multiplying I will multiply you," and so after he had patiently endured, he obtained the promise. For men indeed swear by the greater, and an oath for confirmation is for them an end to all dispute. Thus God determining to show more abundantly to the heirs of promise the immutability of his counsel, confirmed it by an oath, that by two immutable things, in which it is impossible for God to lie, we might have strong conciliation who have fled for refuge to lay hold of the hope set before us. This hope we have as an anchor for the soul, both sure and steadfast.

Hebrews 6:13–19 (NKJV)

This tells us we have covenant with God and that he is going to bless us. We hold to this promise from our God as we journey through life. Whether today is filled with sunshine or storm, we know our God loves us unconditionally. He loves us with an unchanging everlasting love and has sworn by His own name to bless us.

As we read in scripture, the nation Israel (the natural seed of Abraham) eventually forfeited the land through disobedience, but even then we find God's heart was a broken heart of love:

For I know the plans I have for you, declares the Lord, plans to prosper you and not to harm you, plans to give you hope and a future. Then you will call upon me and come and pray to me, and I will listen to you. You will seek me and find me when you seek me with all your heart. I will be found of you, declares the LORD.

Jeremiah 29:11–13 (NIV)

Do I take pleasure in the death of the wicked? Declares the Sovereign LORD. Rather am I not pleased when they turn from their way and live?

Ezekiel 18:23 (NIV)

God's heart toward us is stated by Jesus Christ in John 10:10 where he says, "The thief comes only to steal and kill and destroy; I have come that you might have life and have it to the full (NIV). God wants only for us to have life and have it to the full. This is said so well by the apostle John in his third epistle chapter one, verse two: "Beloved, I pray that you may prosper in all things and be in health, just as your soul prospers" (NKJV).

There is no bad in God nor in his intentions for us, and there is no good in the devil and his desires against us. God seeks only to love and to bless while the devil seeks only to rob and to kill. Let's settle in our hearts once and for all, God loves us and his love will never fail!

If we sin, we violate this relationship of love and open the door to the devil. When this happens and we fall back into the enemy camp, we need to immediately turn back to Christ in sorrow and repentance. The same as we need the blood of Jesus to save us we also need his blood to keep us.

My children I write this to you so that you will not sin. But if anybody does sin, we have one who speaks to the Father on our defense—Jesus Christ, the Righteous One. He is the atoning sacrifice for our sins.

1 John 2:1–2 (NIV)

Once we have truly repented and turned from our sin, we are then free to again rest in the love and blessing of God.

So that Christ may dwell in your hearts through faith. And I pray that you, being rooted and established in love, may have power, together with all the saints, to grasp how wide and long and high and deep is the love of Christ, and to know this love that surpasses knowledge—that you may be filled to the measure of all the fullness of God.

Ephesians 3:17–19 (NIV)

One evening, some years ago, as I turned onto the freeway, I noticed a large man trying to catch a ride on the side of the road. I stopped and he squeezed himself into my little car. He looked old and worn, as he stared at me through his tired eyes. As we sped along, I went around another car and said to the guy that maybe if they saw him get out of my car, they might stop and give him a ride. He said, "No, they already passed me once."

I said, "Well, a lot of people are afraid of getting robbed or killed or something."

He said, "I'm not going to do that to you, I've quit.

I used to steal and kill and hurt people, but I'm not that way anymore." Boy was I glad to hear that!

When I got my voice back, for lack of something better to say, I said, "You must be born-again?"

He said, "Yeah." I then felt I had a word from the Spirit about him.

So I asked him, "Which prison were you in?"

He said, "I've been in all of them, I think, from Wisconsin to the coast, but I'm never going back; I've changed." Over the next few miles, as we talked, he made a comment I've never forgotten. He said, "It's easy to believe all these things like the sun and moon and the world being made by God, and it's easy for me to believe Jesus died and God brought him back to life again. All these things make sense. The thing I try to understand in my travels and I think about so much when I'm alone; is how can a God so good, love a man like me?" As the old converted convict got out of my car and walked to the side of the road and as I drove away: I too wondered how a God so great could love a wretch like me.

If we look for the answer to this within ourselves, it's not there; but when we look to God and who he is, we can almost understand. It tells us in Ephesians that, in the ages to come, we will be examples of God's grace and kindness. He showed the world love through Jesus Christ. We must receive this by faith.

If anyone acknowledges that Jesus is the Son of God, God lives in him and he in God. And so we know and rely on the love God has for us. God is love. Whoever lives in love lives in God, and God in him.

1 John 4:15–16 (NIV)

God loves us and we can't change that! We must simply believe it's true and know he died for us because his love was so great! He sets us free and then with blood stained brow and nail scarred hands asks in love, "Will you follow me?"

The Body

After reading the New Testament, we see clearly how being born-again is more than a change of mind and a new philosophy; it's an entirely new lifestyle. We are to see ourselves in a new way, as a member of the family known as the Body of Christ, the church.

The manifestation of the church in our community is what we call the local church. It is in this atmosphere of family that we live out the selfless love Christ has put in our hearts. The church isn't the building we meet in, but rather the Body of Christ made up of the believers. Let's look at a couple of verses about this:

> I write so that you may know how you ought to conduct yourself in the house of God, which is the church of the living God, the pillar and ground of the truth
>
> 1 Timothy 3:15 (NKJV)

You also as living stones, are built up a spiritual house, a holy priesthood, to offer up spiritual sacrifices, acceptable to God through Jesus Christ.

1 Peter 2:5 (NKJV)

God no longer sees us as we used to be, but rather as members of Jesus' body here on earth. Notice what the following verses say:

"After all, no one ever hated his own body, but he feeds it and cares for it, just as Christ does the church ... for we are members of his body."

Ephesians 5:29–30 (NIV)

And God placed all things under his feet and gave him to be the head over everything for the church, which is his body, the fullness of him who fills everything in every way.

Ephesians 1:22 (NIV)

We are members of the Body of Christ, which is the church. The Scriptures teach us the Body has many members (parts) and yet is still one Body:

Each of us is a part of the one body of Christ. Some of us are Jews, some are Gentile, some are slaves, and some are free. But the Holy Spirit has fitted us all together into one body. We have been baptized into Christ's body by one Spirit, and have all been given that same Holy Spirit. Yes, the body has many parts, not just one part ... Now here is what I am trying to say: All of you together are the one body of Christ, and each one of you is a separate and necessary part of it.

1 Corinthians 12:13–14, 27 (TLB)

When we receive Jesus, he has a place for us in his Body. Without apology, the Word says we are no longer our own, we belong to God. We can't be rightly related to Christ without being rightly related to the church. It needs to be understood that this is not merely an abstract idea. Physically and spiritually, we are to be related to and involved with the Body. We read in the book of Romans:

> I beseech you, therefore, brethren, by the mercies of God that you present your bodies a living sacrifice, holy, acceptable to God, which is your reasonable service.
>
> Romans 12:1 (NKJV)

Notice it says present your bodies, not your agreement, or belief in this concept, but the actual physical involvement of your life in the society of the church.

> And let us consider how we may spur one another toward love and good deeds. Let us not give up meeting together, as some are in the habit of doing, but let us encourage one another—and all the more as you see the Day approaching.
>
> Hebrews 10:24–25 (NIV)

In order for us to grow and become the person God wants us to be, we must become a submitted member of the manifested Body of Christ, the local church. In the local church we find the love of God manifested. Here the love of Jesus is lived out.

This is the message you heard from the beginning: we should love one another... This is how we know what love is: Jesus Christ laid down his life for us. And we ought to lay down our lives for our brothers.

1 John 3:11–16 (NIV)

Beloved, let us love one another, for love is of God and everyone who loves is born of God and knows God. He who does not love does not know God, for God is love. In this the love of God was manifested toward us, that God has sent his only begotten Son into the world, that we might live through him. In this is love, not that we loved God, but that he loved us and sent his Son to be the propitiation for our sins. Beloved, if God so loved us, we also ought to love one another.

1 John 4:7–11 (NKJV)

Let's take a look now at how God intends the Body to function when it comes together:

When you come together, everyone has a hymn, or a word of instruction, a revelation, a tongue or an interpretation. All of these must be done for the strengthening of the church.

1 Corinthians 14:26 (NIV)

We should notice this says everyone, which includes us. If we have received Jesus into our heart, and as we seek to be his disciple, we will be led of the Spirit into our place in the Body.

God calls some of his servants to serve the church in special types of ministry. The Bible speaks of five ministry types given to the church for the work of the ministry in equipping of the saints. These are referred to as "the five-fold ministries" of the church.

> It was he (Jesus) who gave some to be apostles, some to be prophets, some to be evangelists, and some to be pastor's and teachers, to prepare God's people for works of service, so that the body of Christ may be built up until we all reach unity in the faith and in the knowledge of the Son of God and become mature, attaining to the whole measure of the fullness of Christ.
>
> Ephesians 4:11 (NIV, parentheses added)

The Scripture clearly states it is God's plan that these five ministry types be found in the local church until everyone has come to the stature and fullness of Christ. In other words, they will be found ministering among the church until Christ returns or until everyone in the church is like Jesus. The life and power and purposes of our risen Lord are released where these five ministry types are functioning in God's divine order. As a broom sweeps the floor regularly and keeps it clean, so these ministries must be recognized and released to minister to the Body in order for it to be balanced and healthy.

Within the local assembly, we will find deacons and elders. The deacons will be handling the daily administration (working of the church), while the elders will be giving themselves to the ministry of prayer and the Word. (Here again, this should not be an excuse to see some of us as having a more perfect standing/higher place in Christ. We can see by reading the book of Acts, the deacons did as many or more miracles as the original Apostles.) Whether we ever serve in these capacities or not, we should all aspire to mature into the qualification listed for them in the Word.

In Paul's letter to the Romans, we learn how God has a specific place of ministry for us in the church. The Holy Spirit imparts grace (God's enablement) to each of us to function and serve there:

> Just as each of us has one body with many members, and these members do not all have the same function, so in Christ we who are many form one body, and each member belongs to all the others. We have different gifts, according to the grace given us. If a man's gift is prophesying, let him use it in proportion to his faith. If it is serving, let him serve; if it is teaching, let him teach; if it is encouraging, let him encourage; if it is contributing to the needs of others, let him give generously; if it is leadership, let him govern diligently; if it is showing mercy, let him do it cheerfully. Love must be sincere. Hate what is evil; cling to what is good. Be devoted to one another in brotherly love. Honor one another above yourselves. Never be lacking in zeal, but keep your spiritual fervor, serving the Lord.
>
> Romans 12:4–11 (NIV)

This tells us we are a part of the others; it also tells us as we walk in love we are to use our gifts for the building up of the church.

In the church, we will be able to grow up in Jesus, as we submit ourselves to the anointed ministries God has placed there. As we live in relationship with other believers, we come to know the plan and purpose for our lives in him. There is an old saying, "If you want to grow up, you have to show up." This is not only cute; it's true! The same way God ordained for children to grow up in a family, he has ordained for Christians to grow up in the church. As we allow it, our lives are changed and we grow into mature disciples as we move ever deeper into Christ as we function in our place within the Body. We become those who are pleasing to him in every way, bearing fruit and abounding in good works. Once again, I want to encourage you that it isn't a religion it's a relationship.

You must realize that the Body of Christ is never stationary. It can never stand still! The convert of today must become tomorrow's apostle, pastor, teacher, evangelist, and prophet. In the healthy body, you will see the convert come in, grow up, and go out, as the church grows, and goes into all the world. When the Body is functioning rightly, we will find true ministry (this is everybody) and relationship. First the ministry will be upward unto God, then inward among the Body, then outward to the world. It must be in this priority, in right relationship with God, healthy within, then free to reveal Jesus to a lost and dying world. When this is out of divine order you will find confusion and strife; or at best a stagnant dry experience, rather than the life and love of Jesus.

We must find a way to be rightly related to the church of Jesus Christ. I'm saying this as I warn you of the problems you may encounter in the local body from time to time. You need to be aware of this so that when you encounter trouble, you won't become discouraged and withdrawn. There are times in the local body when we experience strife due to immaturity and fleshly activities.

> But if you have bitter envy and selfish ambition in your heart, do not boast about it or deny the truth. Such "wisdom" does not come down from heaven but is earthly, unspiritual, of the devil. For where you have envy and selfish ambition, there you find disorder and ever evil practice.
>
> James 3:14–16 (NIV)

> The Lord does not look at the things man looks at. Man looks at the outward appearance, but the Lord looks at the heart.
>
> 1 Samuel 16:7 (NIV)

It is a tragic reality in the church that men's motives, at times, are not pure. When this happens, we need to look beyond to the God we serve and continue in our personal relationship with Christ and his love. God is doing a perfect work in the midst of an imperfect people. As it tells us in 2 Corinthians 11:3; sometimes the same as Eve was deceived by the devil, people in the church can be too. When there are people who are in the flesh and not obeying the

Spirit, there can be many wounded, which brings them to fall away. We cannot let this happen to us. It is only with much prayer and patience we stay true to God in the midst of the turmoil this causes. During these times, we need to draw very close to the Lord so the Holy Spirit can lead us through the storm. If we have moved away from a personal relationship with Christ into a relationship revolving around others, these times can cause us to give up on God's place and plan for us. We can never allow this to bring us to where we fall out of fellowship and remove ourselves from life in the Body. When we are hurt, we must forgive! When we are wounded, Christ will heal us. When we remain faithful to him, he is honored. I can say from personal experience that it has been during troubled times in the Body that I have found a deeper life in Christ, as I have struggled to find my way through the process.

We need to be careful that we don't become deceived and feel we can serve Jesus apart from being rightly related to the Body. This reminds me of a lady I met some years ago in a small town where I had moved to establish a local church. I had heard of this woman who was said to be a Christian. While in a store one day, I had the opportunity to meet her. As we introduced ourselves and began to talk, I asked her what church she attended. She smiled the sweetest smile and told me she didn't go to church and that her pastor was someone over 2,000 miles away (3,218 kilometers). I then inquired if she had moved to the area from there, or if her pastor had perhaps at one time been in our area.

She answered, "No I've never met the man. I only listen to him on my cassette player." As I invited her to come to our church services, she said, "No, there is just so much trouble when people get together in a local church; I do much better with my "plastic preacher" (her own words). She said she laughed and cried and sent him money and never had to put up with all the stuff that goes on in the local church. I felt sad as I realized she didn't understand that it's in "all the stuff that goes on in the local church" that we love one another and grow up. She was not only missing all God had for her to receive from the Body, but the Body was missing all God had for her to give as well.

Please don't use this to think there is something wrong in receiving from such things as tapes, books, and television ministries. These are a great blessing to us as long as we don't allow them to replace the life of the Body, or to undermine our commitment to what God wants to do here and now with the group we are called to. These ministries are so necessary where a local healthy church isn't established yet.

Many Christians today are very well educated, but are rendered useless simply because they refuse to obey God in the area of submission to the local church. Their aloof manner of intellectually judging everything keeps them from ever doing anything. Instead of producing fruit, they simply remain legends in their own minds. We must not let this happen to us, if we are to grow into the mature vessel

God wants us to become. We need to "join up" and "grow up."

When we are in the local assembly with our brothers and sisters, one of the most sacred and precious times we will ever know is when we join together in partaking of communion. I think the best way to explain this to you is to read what Paul wrote to the early church:

> For I received from the Lord what I also passed on to you: The Lord Jesus, on the night he was betrayed, took bread, and when he had given thanks, he broke it and said, "This is my body, which is for you; do this in remembrance of me." In the same way, after supper he took the cup, saying "this cup is the new covenant of my blood; do this, whenever you drink it, in remembrance of me." For whenever you eat this bread and drink this cup, you proclaim the Lord's death until he comes.
>
> 1 Corinthians 11:23–26 (NIV)

I cannot express the joy and excitement I have when I take communion! I thank God no one stands between me and God at that moment. The blood of Jesus Christ gives me access to the throne of God, and no man can touch this. God has met me there so many times and in so many ways. We can expect him to speak, correct, encourage, deliver, and even heal us as we release our faith to Him during Holy Communion.

Another of the important ministries we find in the local church is the laying on of hands. There is nothing quite as precious as the touch of Jesus through the love of another person as they identify with us. This happens when ministry/individuals of the Body lay their hands on another person for a specific spiritual purpose. This is used in a variety of ways and all of them are found to be in accordance with the scripture. The laying on of hands is used in the Bible as a point of contact for the releasing of faith in the healing of the sick:

> There was an estate nearby that belonged to Publius; the chief official on the island. He welcomed us to his home and for three days entertained us hospitably. His father was sick in bed, suffering from fever and dysentery. Paul went in to see him and after prayer, placed his hands on him and healed him. When this happened, the rest of the sick on the island came and were cured.
>
> Acts 28:7–9 (NIV)

> Is any one of you sick? He should call for the elders of the church to pray over him and anoint him with oil in the name of the Lord. And the prayer offered in faith will make the sick person well; The Lord will raise him up. If he has sinned, he will be forgiven.
>
> James 5:14–15 (NIV)

Even though we know the laying on of hands was common practice in the early church, sometimes people released their faith and healing took place even without it. For example, some were healed by Peter's shadow. Others were healed simply by someone speaking a word. Yet, the common practice was the physical laying on of hands.

Now let's look at some verses where the laying on of hands was used for purposes other than healing:

> Then Ananias went to the house and entered it. Placing his hands on Saul, he said, "Brother Saul, the Lord-Jesus, who appeared to you on the road as you were coming here—has sent me so that you may see again and be filled with the Holy Spirit." Immediately, something like scales fell from Saul's eyes, and he could see again. He got up and was baptized, and after taking some food, he regained his strength.
>
> Acts 9:17–19 (NIV)

> While they were worshiping the Lord and fasting, the Holy Spirit said, "Set apart for me Barnabas and Saul for the work to which I have called them." So after they had fasted and prayed, they placed their hands on them and sent them off.
>
> Acts 13:2–3 (NIV)

> Do not neglect your gift, which was given you through a prophetic message when the body of elders laid their hands on you.
>
> 1 Timothy 4:14 (NIV)

> For this reason I remind you to fan into flame the gift of God, which is in you through the laying on of my hands.
>
> II Timothy 1:6 (NIV)

It is plain to see from these passages that through the laying on of hands, the Spirit of God can be imparted through one person to another. This should take place in the Body, where both the giver and receiver are known and submitted. We should never avail ourselves to this practice through people we don't know to be confirmed, solid ministers of God. In the same regard we should not be quick to lay our hands on someone we don't know.

In the Body, we will experience the laying on of hands and many other gifts and expressions of Jesus with the others. These relationships will not only help us as we walk in love, they will also keep us humble and on course in our walk with Christ.

The Bible tells us knowledge puffs up (pride), but love builds up (1 Corinthians 8:1). Head knowledge does not make us a great disciple; love does. There is no better place to prove this true than in the Body. Any time we think we're exactly like Jesus we are brought to reality in our relationship with the Body. Bible examples of so-called great followers of Jesus in the early church, like Peter who cut off a guard's ear, or Paul and Barnabas disagreeing, show us this is part of maturing. If we are humble enough to allow it, our knowledge is turned into a walk of love, where we esteem others higher than ourselves.

Within the Body, there will be numerous opportunities to minister practically to one another. An example of this fellowship is plainly seen in the book of Acts where it tells how the early Christian believers ate, prayed, and shared together. Jesus always had time within his busy schedule to pick up a child tenderly, or to compassionately heal someone. When we are walking in the Spirit, we will sense his leading us into expressions of love, fellowship, and other kind deeds.

As we live our lives in service to others, we must be careful it is done from relationship and not from duty. We must never allow our good works to become the avenue through which we approach God, or feel that they are what make us acceptable to him. We live in liberty knowing, we are accepted by God through our faith in Jesus Christ. Our good works are simply an expression of our love.

Our love becomes deeper and deeper as we continue to walk with him, being led of the Spirit and living our lives for Christ.

It is God's expectation we develop in our intimacy with him. As we do this we come to the church services or meetings as vessels full of the Spirit ready to be poured out in loving service, rather than showing up empty and drained only to take. It is when we are walking in fellowship with God as individuals we become the mighty Body we are meant to be. I have known many converts and congregations where the people attend for years and all remain babies. They come to church expecting to be spoon fed and allowed to cry, and then leave until next time. As they show up with lives empty of the Word and void of prayer, with no time spent alone with God; they remain undisciplined and unfruitful. It is in our personal relationship with God we find Jesus first, and then we move into the Body to give and receive.

It is of extreme importance for us to be grounded in the Word as an individual when we are looking for a church or moving from one location to another. This will keep us from being blown about by bad teaching when we find a group that doesn't obey the Bible.

No matter how great the church leadership is, they will never accomplish all God has for us and the group. The rest of the Body needs to participate in the release of what the Holy Spirit desires for the church. When this happens, the church is transformed from an organization, to the living organism God desires it to be.

For the full expression of God's grace to be expressed, we must understand God never intended the church to be divided into those who minister and those who don't. It is vitally important we see the church as the living organism, the Body of Christ, where each member has the same value and standing before God. We all stand on level ground before God's Throne. We would never think in a family the father stood closer to God than the mother and the children. We should never see it different concerning the members of the church. While there are some who are called to speaking ministries they are no more important or closer to God than we are. Perfect and complete entrance before the throne of God is received through the imputed righteousness of Jesus Christ. As I've said earlier, our value and acceptance before God is obtained only through faith in the blood sacrifice of Jesus. We are called to be kings and priest unto God (Revelation 1:6). We must never reduce ourselves back to the old Levitical pattern (the Law of Moses) where only a few chosen men stood as mediators between God and the people. The only man we need to mediate between us and God is Christ Jesus! No man or group can stop us from relating directly to our Heavenly Father through Jesus Christ. It is the blood of Jesus alone that brings us to perfect standing before God.

As we stand in this truth, we then must also abide in the truth that there are offices in the church that we need to be rightly related and submitted to. They are given to the church for ministry purposes to build the believers up and not for pre-eminence. Equality for all men before God has been purchased by Christ's blood at the cross and can never be earned. From this equality God elects some to positions of government in the church. We need to recognize them, submit to them and learn from them. We can do this with joy once we rest in the proper understanding of who we are in Christ. Going back to the example of the family, even though the child is equal with the father in value the father maintains authority over the child as he grows up and matures into an adult. So it is in the church.

We must never selfishly desire authority, because we can't do this and at the same time have a servant's heart. We need to yearn for a greater influence for Him not for recognition for ourselves. Our promotion comes from God and not what others see us as being. As God shows us our place in the Body we simply need to respond with a servant's heart and joyfully serve him there.

Once we see position in the church has no relevance to our salvation or standing before God; it removes us from feeling we are less than his best. It also removes every excuse we have for not pressing into God and becoming all he wants us to be. God looks at our heart, not our ministry position.

Our office in the church is an election of grace. It is our position in Christ that gives us authority over the realms of darkness. Many times a holy person with a right relationship with Christ and the church will have a far greater impact for God than someone that is busy in works and lacking in personal relationship.

> Remain in me, and I will remain in you. No branch can bear fruit of itself; it must remain in the vine. Neither can you bear fruit unless you remain in me. I am the vine; you are the branches. If a man remains in me and I in him, he will bear much fruit; apart from me you can do nothing.
>
> John 15:4–5 (NIV)

We should never feel like anyone is closer to God than we are. At the same time we must not think, "It's just Jesus and me and I am free." God clearly expects us to be in a church, submitted to those around us and to the ministry he has placed over us. As we submit to the ministry God has placed in the church, we can receive from the gifts God has placed there. Here we find ourselves being built up together in love.

> You also as living stones, are being built into a spiritual house to be a holy priesthood, offering spiritual sacrifices acceptable to God through Jesus Christ...But you are a chosen people, a royal priesthood, a holy nation, a people belonging to God, that you may declare the praises of him who called you out of darkness into his marvelous light. Once you were not a people, but now you are the people of God; once you had not received mercy, but now you have received mercy.
>
> 1 Peter 2:5–9, 10 (NIV)

The greatest calling any of us will ever know is the perfect place of grace we rest in as we go ever deeper in Christ. It is our relationship with him that releases God's Spirit to us and through us. We must abide in relationship with him and rest there (in grace) as he builds his church through us.

It is up to God and not us to choose what our calling is. If we do not understand and believe this we will continue struggling in finding our place. Any time we see authority in the church as being related to our value or standing before God; we will always be looking for a way to relate to God out of works. This causes us to be self-serving and competitive instead of serving in love. We must see Christ as the head of the church and the Holy Spirit as the administrator and all of us whether apostle or greeter, are simply servants. When this is violated by man, we have dead works and the Spirit is quenched among us. This is why we should seek only God's glory as we seek an ever-greater influence for him.

Jesus called them together and said, "You know that the rulers of the Gentiles lord it over them, and their high officials exercise authority over them. Not so with you. Instead, whoever wants to become great among you must be your servant, and whoever wants to be first must be your slave—just as the Son of Man did not come to be served, but to serve, and to give his life a ransom for many."

Matthew 20:25–28 (NIV)

We must be very careful to always maintain a servant's heart toward the Body and our place in it. We need to be reminded again and again how not only the elders but all of the believers stand on the same level with God, and every one of us needs to raise up out of the natural realm into the realm of the Spirit. Only when the church begins to meet and function on the higher level of the Spirit will we see the fullness of Christ in our midst. This is true whether we are in a home group or a larger church setting. No matter what style we meet in we must have the Holy Spirit in order for the Body of Christ to be the living organism God intends it to be.

Too often, the church service consists of only a few being yielded to the Holy Spirit enough to sense what Jesus would have for the Body at that exact place and time. The service then amounts to no more than the song service and the message reaching out to the people, trying to get them out of themselves and into the Spirit. This may or may not be accomplished by the end of the service. Instead of the Body having come together and functioning as it should, the members have simply come in filled with self to be bottle-fed enough to get them through another week of self-seeking. Out of this the church never comes to fulfill the mind and purpose of Christ.

We must walk in relationship with Christ so when we, the Body come together, Christ Jesus (in the presence of the Holy Spirit) is in our midst. God is there and he has a plan for the service. This should be like the joyous happy time when the parents come home and the children are excited and happy and it is a wonderful time of fellowship as everyone gathers in love. As each member yields to the administrator (Holy Spirit—mind of Christ) the potential for the power of Jesus to meet every need is among us. The fullness of Jesus and his miraculous works are then seen and greater things than he has done are done among us. As the gifts and moving of the Holy Spirit are released in our midst, Jesus is made real and glorified.

> "Again I tell you that if two of you on earth agree about anything you ask for, it will be done for you by my father in heaven. For where two or three come together in my name, there am I with them."
>
> Matthew 18:19–20 (NIV)

The Spirit of God not only needs to be released in the worship, but the Gifts of the Spirit need to be released through each of us as individual believers. As the church becomes one vessel submitted in the soul and intellectual realm to the Spirit, the power of Christ is released as God intends it to be. We aren't waiting on God—God is waiting on us.

God commands us to grow in the grace and the knowledge of Jesus Christ. We shouldn't allow ourselves to become out of balance and grow in our head knowledge and fail to grow in our relationship of grace. The extreme of this is seen in the Pharisees who felt they had total knowledge of God, while at the same time they didn't even recognize Jesus as he stood there among them.

If we don't walk in relationship, we can have the right understanding, but still not be someone who walks in the power and potential God wants for us. We will find our time at a meeting as being no more than our relating to others who are in the same place we are. We will make a mental agreement with the truth of the message. We will try to apply it to our own selfish needs. But will we ever really know the reality and life God wants for us? Will the presence and power of God be there, or will we talk about the weather, family, and other common things, instead of being in the presence of our God? Fellowship with believers is important, but not in comparison to finding the presence of God. When we see head knowledge as the way to God, instead of the release of the power of the Holy Spirit through us it has a negative influence on others. Knowledge of God is good when it brings us into a deeper relationship, but it is detrimental when it begins to replace our dependence on the Holy Spirit with self-sufficiency. Many times someone with more head knowledge may impress people, but not God. When standing before God is seen as being determined by how much we have learned the young believer begins to feel unqualified because they get the impression they don't know enough to do anything for God. I am not against education; I wish we all had more of it. I am concerned in what education can produce in causing us to intellectually pursue God, while denying the moving of the Holy Spirit and the power of the cross. We are in error when we try to move the church forward out of intellectual excellence rather than by the Spirit. The reason we don't have the power of Christ among us many times is because we have quenched the Spirit with our intellectual pursuit of his grace. The church needs to mature in the Spirit to the place where the Holy Spirit is in control and not the intellect of man. Then as one unit the church can walk with the Spirit and produce the fruit God intends for it.

Perhaps not all of us will be called to a "fivefold ministry" but we are all called to minister and to receive the outpouring of the Holy Spirit. There is no limit to how much each of us can live and move in the Spirit of God, if we will just pay the price of living for him. How can we not pay the price when we consider what he has done for us?

Some of the most profound things God will ever do will be done through the humble disciple as they live the crucified life before the throne of grace. Jesus makes mention of this in Matthew 11:25–27 (NKJV):

> At that time Jesus answered and said, "I thank you, Father, Lord of heaven and earth, that you have hidden these things from the wise and prudent and have revealed them to babes. Even so, Father, for it seemed good in your sight. All things have been delivered to me by My Father, and no one knows the Son except the Father, nor does anyone know the Father except the Son, and the one to whom the Son will to reveal him."

I pray you will never give up or let go of God's plan and place for you in him. There is a natural tendency to look at ourselves in the natural and not in the Spirit. This causes us to always feel too inadequate to move in the Spirit with God. We must crucify and overcome this and know we are a new creation in Christ ordained to good works. Never quit believing this and never give up on yourself.

> But we have this treasure in jars of clay to show that this all-surpassing power is from God and not from us.
>
> 2 Corinthians 4:7 (NIV)

> But he said to me, "My grace is sufficient for you, for my power is made perfect in weakness." Therefore I will boast all the more gladly about my weakness, so that Christ's power may rest on me.
>
> 2 Corinthians 12:9 (NIV)

We must never let anyone or anything rob us of our potential in God. Is anything too difficult for God? No! We're not even too much for him. God has a destiny for you in his kingdom and his church, and it's a lot bigger than you can ever realize in your natural mind. Never-never-never give up! He who has begun this good work in you will complete it!

Giving

God loved us so much he gave his only begotten Son, so we could be forgiven and saved. Jesus lived on this earth to reveal this love to you and me. Every person he touched was an act of love from God to man. Christ's death was the supreme act of love. It cost him his life-blood to purchase the way back to God for you and I; he now sits at the right hand of the Father and in his love he is praying for us. Let's read 2 Corinthians 5:14–5 (NIV).

> For Christ's love compels us, because we are convinced that one died for all, and therefore all died. And he died for all, that those who live should no longer live for themselves, but for him who died for them and was raised again.

It is through the selfless love of Jesus that we find the courage to trust God and give ourselves completely to him. We no longer live for ourselves, but for him who died for us. Faith allows us to know the very best place we will ever be is at the foot of the cross, in total surrender. We come to know and trust God as not only the Creator, but also the possessor of the heavens and the earth. He is the one true source of all things concerning us and our lives.

To help you in this, I need to talk to you about money. I know this is an area we all need to be right in, because if you're not right in your pocketbook, you are not right in your heart. I'm glad I am not being paid as a minister, so you can know my motives are pure in this. I will tell you about my own experiences and then we'll look at the scriptures.

When I knelt and asked Jesus to forgive me and come into my heart, I was surprised when the room filled with his presence. There on the floor he met me, a drunken wretch in my need. In the following days, I came to realize the selflessness of a God so Holy, who would humble himself and come to a wicked man like me and translate me out of darkness into his light. I was filled with joy at the peace I had, but was also afraid I might slip and go back to my life of sin. Somewhere during this time I heard the following verse quoted:

> Do not store up for your-selves treasure on earth, where moth and rust destroy, and where thieves break in and steal. But store up for your-selves treasures in heaven, where moth and rust do not destroy, and where thieves do not break in and steal. For where your treasure is, there your heart will be also.
>
> Matthew 6:19–21 (NIV)

I realized if I gave my finances to God, my heart would remain true to him too. You see, giving our money is simply letting our heart talk through our purse. I loved him and wanted to continue loving him all my life, so I began a life of giving. In the beginning, I didn't know how much to give, so I just gave him everything and asked him what I was supposed to take back. It wasn't until later I learned about giving ten percent and how those who do will be blessed in return.

We give to God in faith knowing that he is the one true source: not our job, our savings, our own abilities, nor any other thing. We trust him as God alone to meet our every need. The Bible tells us in Philippians, 4:19, that God will supply all of our needs according to his riches in glory by Christ Jesus. It is in our giving we release his hand to bless us indeed!

One night in church, they were passing the offering plate and as it came toward me I looked in my billfold and saw I had a one dollar bill and a twenty dollar bill. I had hoped for a five, but I didn't have one. I began to argue with myself which one I should give. First, I pulled out the dollar and felt guilty; then I put it back and got out the twenty, but I then felt that was too much. I was in business at the time and this was all the money I had to give. The bank account was depleted and I didn't know when I'd have anymore. As the plate got closer and closer, I suddenly realized Jesus gave his all for me. So I decided to give both bills and release my faith that God would meet my needs. When I went to the mailbox the next day, there was nine hundred and seventy-two dollars in it! Jesus had met me at the point of my need and in this I experienced relationship with him.

People say we shouldn't give to get back. The reality shouldn't be ignored, however, that in giving, we do so to a living and powerful God. It is in this area of giving, and seeing God meet our daily provision, we develop our personal relationship with him. Here we realize he wants to be God among us, and not just an uncaring master above us:

> Give, and it shall be given unto you. A good measure, pressed down, shaken together and running over, will be poured into your lap. For with the same measure you use, it will be measured to you.
>
> Luke 6:38 (NIV)

We can approach God with one of two attitudes concerning money. One is we give and receive in relationship with God, he blesses us, and we have more to serve him with. The other is instead of us serving God; we give so God can help us serve our money and selfish desires. If we aren't careful, we begin to build a life of trying to manipulate God into serving us instead of us serving him.

> "No one can serve two masters. Either he will hate the one and love the other, or he will be devoted to the one and despise the other. You cannot serve both God and money."
>
> Matthew 6:24 (NIV)

Our giving is motivated by the example of Jesus Christ and by our faith God will bless us and meet our needs in return. There is nothing wrong with wealth; it is our attitude towards it that matters the most to God.

Let's look at a couple other experiences where God rewarded the giver, and then we will look at another scripture on this. When I moved to Valier, Montana, to establish a church there, the men had a meeting concerning how I was to be paid. In the church, there was a box in the back that had two slots in the top. One was marked tithe and the other was marked offering. No one ever passed the plate or asked for money. The people, of their own free-will, would put the money in the box as God directed their hearts. After some discussion, I said I would take ninety percent of what came from the tithe side of the box. I said I wanted to give the other ten percent to ministry outside the group. One fellow, in disbelief, asked if I was crazy. In the six months the church had been in existence before I arrived, the average monthly income for both tithe and offering had been only four hundred dollars. This amount was not enough for the rent and food for my family. I said I was not crazy, but believed when we walk with God, he will walk with us. The decision was made to move forward under this agreement. Within twelve months, we had a church finished, a school in place, and my family's needs were met.

A few weeks later, we had another meeting where I said we needed to add room to the sanctuary. The same man who had previously asked if I were crazy took the last two hundred and fifty dollars he had to his name and gave it to start the project. The next week, after having no work for quite some time, an oil company from some miles away called him to come to work for them. He worked for sixty hours for sixty dollars an hour. This provided him with the money to keep his family fed and in their house until spring work was available.

I also remember the night a lady stood up at the close of a service and confessed she needed money for the landlord or she was going to be evicted from the house she was living in. One of the brothers, who had been out of work with very little money left, gave his last few dollars so she wouldn't have to move out. The next week, he went back to work and stayed busy for the rest of the winter.

I have found when we are financially in need and don't know what to do we need to give from what we have left, look up, and worship God. This will release our faith to him. He's real! He's alive! God cares for his own. There is not enough room in this book for me to tell of all the times I have needed finances and out of my need I have given a part of it as a seed of my faith. As I have sown it I have released my faith. Again and again, consistently, God has met my need and lifted me beyond where I would have been had I not trusted him.

Now let's look at this scripture about giving. It starts way back with our father Abraham in the book of Genesis.

Then Melchizedek king of Salem brought out bread and wine. He was the priest of God Most High, and he blessed Abram, saying, "Blessed be Abram by God Most High, Creator of heaven and earth. And blessed be God Most High, who delivered your enemies into your hand," Then Abram gave him a tenth of everything.

Genesis 14:18–23 (NIV)

We see Abraham wasn't required to give this way. He was never asked to give it. He just had so much love and worship for God he couldn't help but give. This is the same as when God loved us so much he became a man and died on the cross for us.

Giving money doesn't have anything to do with buying a place before God or keeping him from punishing us if we don't. It has to do with us loving him and wanting a living relationship. I believe what we do with our money expresses where we are in our heart. When God said he loved a cheerful giver, I think he was saying I love your open heart toward me and the way you trust me to meet your needs.

We should never transfer our standing before God away from the cross to works of the flesh such as our giving. We need to be like Abraham, who after receiving God's blessing turned in worship and gave a tithe of all he had.

We find under the old covenant God said give and then I will bless you. In Jesus Christ, God has already blessed us. We no longer give in fear, we give in faith. This releases what is already ours in Christ. As New Testament Christians our giving doesn't change our standing before God's throne; it simply opens our heart and our faith. This in turn releases God's grace to flow down and meet all our needs in Christ Jesus. The blessings that come to us from our giving come as we release our faith in the cross of Christ and the riches that were provided through his sacrifice.

When we as a disciple of Jesus give, we simply rest before the throne of grace and as Abraham we give our tithes and offerings in worship to our God. It is here we surrender our future well being, the fruit of our labors, and the desires of our heart. In our giving we confess to our God, "You are creator of Heaven and Earth, possessor of all things now and forever. You alone are God to me."

Prayer

Have you ever had a place where you could go, and there everything seemed to make sense? When I was a boy it was the "big hill." When things got to pressing in, I would take my backpack and rifle and head for the big hill. My destination was about a mile and a half west of the house I grew up in. This hill wasn't anything special to anyone but me. As I walked across the hay fields and up toward the timber with Sooner, my dog, it seemed like I was finding myself again. There I would make a shelter out of pine boughs, build a fire, and be alone with my dreams and hurts. I would sit and watch the fire and eat some stew. As the fire danced, the dog slept, and I surveyed the world from my hill, it seemed life would again get to the point I could handle it. I never was quite sure why, because nothing ever really changed except maybe my attitude. Prayer is the place I go now and find my peace. In prayer, a lot more than just our attitude changes! It is in prayer we meet with our personal God.

> He gives power to the weak, and to those who have no might he increases strength. Even the youths shall faint and be weary, and the young men shall utterly fall, but those who wait on the Lord shall renew their strength; they shall mount up with wings of eagles, they shall run and not be weary, they shall walk and not faint.
>
> Isaiah 40:29–31 (NKJV)

Prayer is where we come to the presence of God himself and find his plan, deliverance, and power. Here we praise and worship him for all he is and all he has done, and will do. The only ones that know this place of relationship are those who approach God through Jesus Christ.

In our communion with God, our praying can take many forms, the same as a conversation with one another can. We do have an example of prayer Jesus gave:

> In this manner therefore, pray: Our Father (loving relationship) in heaven, Hallowed be Your name (reverence and worship). Your kingdom come. Your will be done (asking for his direction and guidance) on earth as it is in heaven (submission to his Lordship). Give us this day our daily bread (prayer for personal needs/petition). And forgive us our debts, (confession and repentance) as we forgive our debtors (prayer and forgiveness for others/intercession). And do not lead us into

temptation, (supplication) But deliver us from the evil one (protection). For yours is the kingdom and the power and the glory forever (adoration and acknowledgement). Amen. (agreement)
Matthew 6:9–13 (NKJV, parentheses added)

During the eighteenth century, at the time of the Civil War in the United States, there was an older couple who were very wealthy. They had only one son to love and to give all they had to. As the war drew on, their love for the African-American slaves grew so great they became willing to risk all their love and dreams by sending their only son to join in the conflict. As he disappeared into the distance, they could only hope the war would end soon and he would return in victory.

With anxious hearts they waited for each letter to come and tell them their son had survived another day in the war. The letters were frequent and spoke of the time when he would know the joy again of being home with his loved ones, back in his inheritance, and in fellowship with them. Then one day what they feared most happened—the letters stopped. As days turned into weeks and weeks to months, they waited with no word from their son. The war ended and life went on with nothing left but memories. One day, the father heard loud noises and arguing out on the porch of their large home. When he went to the door, he found the butler in heated debate with a ragged beggar, who would not leave. He was waving an old torn piece of paper and demanding to talk to the owner. The father spoke to the butler to allow the man to approach. The stranger came and knelt before the father and handed him the tattered page. The father took the crumpled and blood stained note and read the message it held. "Dear father, I am dying today on the battlefield. I have given my all to purchase freedom for my friends. One of them kneels beside me today helping me with my wounds. If he should ever come to you with this note sealed in my blood; Father, let my riches become his, the same as the price of his freedom has now become mine."

> For you know the grace of our Lord Jesus Christ, that though he was rich, yet for your sakes he became poor, so that you through his poverty might become rich.
>
> II Corinthians 8:9 (NIV)

> In that day you will no longer ask me anything. I tell you the truth, my Father will give you whatsoever you ask in my name. Ask and you will receive, and your joy will be complete ... In that day you will ask in my name. I am not saying that I will ask the Father on your behalf. No, the Father himself loves you because you have loved me and have believed that I came from God.
>
> John 16:23–24, 26–27 (NIV)

This is how it is when we are in Jesus. All the riches of heaven are at our disposal. Our faith in the blood; shed by our Savior sets us free from our sins and grants us access to the Father. There before his throne we have relationship with him. The riches of the kingdom are ours through the prayer of faith. It's in prayer we come to the throne of our Creator and rest as royalty, clean and free in Christ. Here we release the power and life of God into our circumstances and the circumstances of others. Let's look at some scripture on this:

> Let us then approach the throne of grace with confidence, so we may receive mercy and find grace to help us in our time of need.
>
> Hebrews 4:16 (NIV)

> Do not be anxious about anything, but in everything, by prayer and petition with thanksgiving, present your request to God.
>
> Philippians 4:6 (NIV)

> Jesus replied, "I tell you the truth, if you have faith and do not doubt, not only can you do what has been done to the fig tree, but you also can say to this mountain, Go throw yourself into the sea, and it will be done, If you believe you will receive whatever you ask for in prayer"
>
> Matthew 21:21–22 (NIV)

> Ask, and it shall be given you; seek, and ye shall find; knock, and it shall be opened unto you: For everyone that asketh, receiveth; and he that seeketh findeth; and to him that knocketh it shall be opened. Or what man is there of you, whom if his son ask bread, will he give him a stone? Or if he ask a fish, will he give him a serpent? Of ye then, being evil know how to give good gifts unto your children, how much more shall your Father which is in heaven give good things to them that ask him?
>
> Matthew 7:7–11 (KJV)

When we look at the Bible with an honest heart, we find anything God is capable of doing, he has promised to do in answer to our prayer. This is so amazing it is more than we can understand without the Spirit's help.

We need to guard our heart and our intentions when we are before the throne of God in prayer. Before you pray, you need to ask yourself, am I praying to the God of my convenience or am I surrendering myself to the Lord of my life? Let's look at a scripture that speaks to us about our attitude in prayer now that we see the availability of this power toward us:

> You attitude should be the same as that of Jesus Christ: who being in very nature God, did not consider equality with God something to be grasped, but made himself nothing, taking the very nature of a servant, being made in human likeness. And being found in appearance as a man, he humbled himself and became obedient unto death—even death on a cross!
>
> Philippians 2:5–8 (NIV)

We who are born-again in Christ actually have the power of the Creator available here on earth. This isn't something we need to struggle with; we just need to believe it, in faith. We then need to turn to the cross, and in humility surrender it all back to him. This is where the Spirit must control us, not the fleshly nor the intellectual realm. If our primary goal in praying isn't an ever-increasing intimacy with the

Almighty, we will pray out of our own self-will and flesh. We will find ourselves asking God for things and not receiving them. We read of this in James 4:3 (NIV). "When you ask, you do not receive, because you ask with wrong motives, that you may spend what you get on your pleasures."

It is critical we never take the power of God and seek to waste it to serve our old nature in the lust of the flesh. Some believe once you are born-again, you then take the power of God and go create your own world of prosperity with your prayer of faith. This is true if you are dead to self and alive to the will of God; but if we are not surrendered to his Lordship, we are actually trying to get God to serve our rebellion. When we are doing this we are still eating of the Tree of the Knowledge of Good and Evil, and aren't walking in the Spirit. We might get a few blessings out of God this way (he makes it rain on the just and the unjust), but we will miss out on the relationship of intimacy God desires to have with us. This is so pitiful when we compare this attitude with the heart of Jesus. He said in John 6:38 (NIV), "For I have come down from heaven not to do my will but to do the will of him who sent me."

Here again, we shouldn't think of the prayer of faith as the starting gun, and go running off to do great things while only checking in with God from time to time. There is nothing worse than taking Christ and making his grace serve our own ambition and selfishness. This is a tragedy we must be careful we are never a part of. We need to realize our relationship with him is the greatest benefit any of us will ever receive from prayer. Let's always remember the admonition of Colossians 3:1–3 (NKJV).

> If then you were raised with Christ, seek those things which are above, where Christ is, sitting on the right hand of God. Set your mind on things above, not on things on the earth. For you died, and your life is hidden with Christ in God.

We can see what we desire outside of Christ is simply evil desire and we need to confess this as sin.

I'll tell you a sad story about myself in this area and pray you will never be this foolish. It started with me learning to fly. It wasn't long before I began to look at the airplanes and wish I had one. Being a person whose mind at that time was not totally seeking "things above," I began to covet a plane of my own. I then began to let the deceiver (devil) tell me I was a son of God and so I deserved one. (Remember what the devil told Jesus? If you are the Son of God command these stones to be made bread.) After all, aren't we "King's Kids?" Shouldn't we have good things? And so it went until I heard somewhere if you confess your prayer and speak out loud, then it will come forth. I prayed, confessed and spoke out loud until sure enough, I got the plane! The lust of my eyes and the pride of life were satisfied. All was well for a time. I soon found God's Word true, however, where it says in Psalms 106:15 (NKJV): "And he gave them their requests, but sent leanness into their souls." You see, I had become so worldly in my heart,

I had begun to want the blessings of God more than I wanted God himself. I realized I was outside the will of God the second time I flew the plane. I got out of it, repented, and got rid of the plane. I prayed for God's forgiveness and grace for my covetousness, which in his eyes was idolatry. It wasn't long after this I read Psalms 12:4 (NKJV): "Who have said, with our lips we will prevail; our lips are our own; who is Lord over us?" We can believe, confess, and testify, but if we are asking for things outside of God's will from our own fleshly desires, we are still in sin.

As we live in intimacy with God and as the Spirit leads, we release our faith and obtain all God has for us. We must have a personal open relationship with him so we can express our desires and allow him to show us his will and purpose. Once we know his will we then move forward as we birth his answer to our prayer by faith. It is here in this arena we inherit the promises as we believe, confess, testify, and praise him for the answer. We speak! The mountain moves! To God be the glory! Amen!

We need to pray in agreement with the Word of God. Then we can be sure it is the will of God for us and for our lives. The Bible is full of promises that are ours as we seek God's will in prayer.

The most important thing for us is to pray. There are a thousand reasons not to, but the worst prayer is a lot better than no prayer at all. We need to know there is no relationship between someone we never talk to. This is true with God as well as man. Jesus said:

But when you pray, go into your room, close the door and pray to your father, who is unseen. Then your Father who sees what is done in secret, will reward you.

Matthew 6:6 (NIV)

We need to make sure we always invite the Holy Spirit to help us as we pray. If we take the time to wait, we will find ourselves being led of the Spirit in our prayer times. There will be times where you feel the need to pray for someone or something, and find out later there was a very real need at just that time for your prayers.

Another part of prayer is fasting. This is when we go without food and sometimes even water as we wrestle in prayer. As we study scripture, we find that not only God, but also angels move in response to our prayer and fasting. There are four times in the Bible where long periods of prayer are talked about besides at Pentecost. They are Daniel, Jesus, the early church praying for Peter, and Paul. We find when Daniel fasted and prayed, an angel came to him. When Jesus had finished his temptation in the wilderness, angels came and ministered to him. When the early church prayed for Peter who was in jail, an angel came and delivered him. When Paul fasted and prayed in the midst of a storm on the sea, after many days an angel came and stood by him.

When we become earnest in prayer, the God who created the universe humbles himself and moves the resources of heaven in our behalf. It is almost more than we can understand. Now that we are in Christ we actually share in the commissioning of angels and the creative power of God!

It is in prayer, as we release our faith, we do battle against the spirit realms of darkness and receive dominion over situations and circumstances. This power is ours as we stand in the authority of Jesus Christ. The devil and all his demons fear and tremble when the church gets on its knees and begins to move the kingdom of God forward against him. Let me encourage you in this time of your beginning days of walking with God to develop a lifestyle of fasting and prayer.

The Enemy

The devil? You mean that cute little guy with the tiny horns, who goes around in red pajamas and carries a pitchfork, that impish little fellow who can't hurt anyone? No! He's the one who has deceived us into thinking he's cute and harmless. He's the enemy of our souls! He's the one Jesus spoke of in John 10:10 where he said, "The thief comes only to steal and to kill and to destroy." He's the one the Bible calls, "the accuser of the brethren," who hates our loving Father and delights in killing his children. It's time we go to the Word again and see what the Bible says about who the devil really is.

> You were the model of perfection, full of wisdom and perfect in beauty, you were in Eden, the garden of God; every precious stone adorned you: ruby, topaz, and emerald, chrysolite, onyx, and jasper, sapphire, turquoise, and beryl. Your settings and mountings were made of gold; on the

day you were created they were prepared. You were anointed as a cherub, for so I ordained you. You were on the holy mount of God; you walked among the fiery stones. You were blameless in your ways from the day you were created till wickedness was found in you. Through your widespread trade you were filled with violence, and you sinned. So I drove you in disgrace from the mount of God, and I expelled you O guardian cherub, from among the fiery stones. Your heart became proud on account of your beauty, and you corrupted your wisdom because of your splendor. So I threw you to the earth; I made a spectacle of you before kings.

Ezekiel 28:12–17 (NIV)

You said in your heart I will ascend into heaven; I will raise my throne above the stars of God; I will sit enthroned on the mount of assembly, on the utmost heights of the sacred mountain. I will ascend above the tops of the clouds; I will make myself like the most high. But you are brought down to the grave, to the depths of the pit.

Isaiah 14:13–15 (NIV)

There was a time in eternity past when Satan was in heaven as an angel of God. When he exalted himself as God, he was judged and cast out of heaven. It tells us in Revelation chapter twelve that Satan was cast out of heaven and one third of the angels fell with him. Jesus spoke of this in Luke 10:18 when he said, "I saw Satan fall as lightning from heaven."

Satan is real in the world we live in today, where

he still seeks to exalt himself. The same as God is totally good and there is no bad in him, Satan is totally bad and there is no good in him. He seeks to keep mankind enslaved in sin and deception and at enmity with God.

> The god of this age (the devil) has blinded the minds of unbelievers, so that they cannot see the light of the gospel of the glory of Christ. Who is the image of God.
>
> 2 Corinthians 4:4 (NIV) (parenthesis added)

> Satan himself masquerades as an angel of light. It is not surprising, then, if his servants masquerade as servants of righteousness.
>
> 2 Corinthians 11:14–15 (NIV)

> He who does what is sinful is of the devil.
>
> 1 John 5:19 (NIV)

> You belong to your father the devil, and you want to carry out your father's desire. He was a murderer from the beginning not holding to the truth, for there is no truth in him. When he lies he speaks his native language, for he is a liar and the father of lies.
>
> John 8:44 (NIV)

> As for you, you were dead in your transgressions and sins, in which you used to live when you followed the ways of this world and the ruler of the kingdom of the air (the devil), the spirit that now works in those who are disobedient. All of us also lived among them at one time, gratifying

the cravings of our sinful nature and following its desires and thoughts. Like the rest, we were by nature objects of wrath.

Ephesians 2:2–3 (NIV) (parenthesis added)

When we are born again and receive Jesus Christ as our personal Savior, we are no longer children of the devil, but we then become the children of God.

He that commiteth sin is of the devil; for the devil sinneth from the beginning. For this purpose the Son of God was manifested, that he might destroy the works of the devil.

1 John 3:8 (KJV)

Since the children (you and I) have flesh and blood, he (Jesus) too shared our humanity so that by his death he might destroy him who holds the power of death—that is the devil—and free those who all their lives were held in slavery by their fear of death.

Hebrews 2:14–15 (NIV) (parenthesis added)

When you are saved, you are redeemed by the blood of Christ out of the darkness into God's kingdom of light. This determines our destiny/eternity. Those who remain in darkness will perish with Satan at the end of this age.

When Christ was crucified and rose again, he triumphed over Satan and all his cohorts, making a show of them openly, triumphing over them by rising from the dead and ascending to the Father in heaven. Jesus tells us in Revelation 1:17–18 (NIV): "Do not be afraid, I am the first and the last. I am the living one, I was dead, and behold I am alive forever and ever! I hold the keys of death and Hades."

Today we find ourselves caught in a battle between two opposing kingdoms. The kingdom of God found within the realm of Jesus Christ and the church, and the kingdom of Satan found around us in this fallen world of sin and suffering. This will continue until the end of the age when Satan is finally destroyed forever.

> Then I heard a loud voice in heaven say: "now have come the salvation and the power and the kingdom of our God, and the authority of his Christ. For the accuser of our brothers who accuses them before our God day and night has been hurled down. They overcame him by the blood of the Lamb and the word of their testimony."
>
> Revelation 12:10–11 (NIV)

> The devil, who deceived them, was cast into the lake of fire and brimstone where the beast and the false prophet are. And they will be tormented day and night forever and ever.
>
> Revelation 20:10 (NIV)

When we came to Jesus and accepted him as our Savior, we were translated out of the kingdom of darkness into God's marvelous kingdom where we now have relationship with him. The dominion Satan held over us was broken. We can, by the Blood of the Lamb and the word of our testimony, overcome him. As we live in this hostile land we battle the realms of darkness and obtain the inheritance that is ours in Jesus Christ. We do this by our faith and our confession as we walk in holiness with our God.

The Fight

Some years ago, when my son Doug was about ten or eleven, we were driving home from school having one of our man-to-man chats. He said something I have never forgotten; "Dad, when I obey you and God, I feel good on the inside, but I have trouble on the outside. And when I do what the other kids want me to do, I have peace on the outside, but I have trouble on the inside." I'm sure you are also finding this to be true since you've come to know Jesus. Perhaps it seems like there is a struggle going on since you have been saved? Well, you are right because there is. Take a look at the following verses:

> Fight the good fight of faith; take hold of the eternal life to which you are called.
>
> 1 Timothy 6:12 (NAS)

> Be self-controlled and alert. Your enemy the devil prowls around like a roaring lion looking for

someone to devour. Resist him, standing firm in the faith, because you know that your brothers throughout the world are undergoing the same kind of suffering.

1 Peter 5:8–9 (NIV)

Finally be strong in the Lord and in his mighty power. Put on the full armor of God so that you can take your stand against the devil's schemes. For our struggle is not against flesh and blood, but against the rulers, against the authorities, against powers of this dark world and against the spiritual forces of evil in the heavenly realms.

Ephesians 6:10–12 (NIV)

We, by our faith, walk in victory. Let's look at some verses on this and then we will talk about it some more.

In which you also were raised with him through faith in the working of God, who raised him from the dead … having disarmed principalities and powers, he made a public spectacle of them, triumphing over them in it.

Colossians 2:12–15 (NKJV)

Through the resurrection of Jesus Christ, who has gone into heaven and is at the right hand of God, angels and authorities and powers having been made subject to him.

1 Peter 3:21–22 (NKJV)

Jesus Christ destroyed the power of the devil over us when he arose from the dead. The dominion

Jesus now has is available to us once we are born-again into the body of Christ. I pray the same as Paul prayed for the church at Ephesus that you might see this. Let's read his prayer together.

> Therefore I also, after I heard of your faith in the Lord Jesus and your love for all the saints, do not cease to give thanks for you, making mention of you in my prayers; that the God of our Lord Jesus Christ, the Father of glory, may give to you the spirit of wisdom and revelation in the knowledge of him, the eyes of your understanding being enlightened, that you may know what is the hope of his calling, what are the riches of the glory of his inheritance in the saints, and what is the exceeding greatness of his power toward us who believe, according to the working of his mighty power which he worked in Christ when he raised him from the dead and seated him at his right hand in the heavenly places, far above all principality and power and might and dominion, and every name that is named, not only in this age but also in that which is to come. And he put all things under his feet, and gave him to be head over all things to the church, which is his body, the fullness of him who fills all in all.
>
> Ephesians 1:15–23 (NKJV)
>
> And raised us up together, and made us sit together in heavenly places in Christ Jesus.
>
> Ephesians 2:6 (NKJV)

We see from this when Christ arose from the dead; God placed the devil and all of his authority under Jesus' feet. When we receive Christ as our personal Savior, we are placed in his Body. This means we too share in the dominion of Christ over the darkness as we abide in him. Jesus, following the resurrection not only took his place at the right hand of the Father, but he also became the head of the church. Now that we are in his Body (the church) we fit somewhere between his head and his feet. All dominion was placed under his feet (the church being his Body) so now as we abide in his Body we too have dominion over the devil and his realm. We appropriate this by our faith in the finished work of Christ's blood, shed at the cross.

The same way God has a beautiful plan for you now, which will end in heaven, so the devil had a plan for you which would have ended in hell. He was satisfied to leave you alone as long as you kept going his way. He had you so deceived before you got saved you didn't even know he was your father at that time. All the good you did, he helped you with, because he was even using that goodness to convince other people they didn't need Jesus. Once you received Christ, you robbed him of his plan for you and he now desires to stop you from taking anything else back from him and his kingdom. Satan does this by trying to destroy us from the inside through sin and by robbing us of our faith. Let's look at the temptation of Jesus and see how the devil works:

> Then Jesus, being filled with the Holy Spirit,
> returned from the Jordan and was led by the Spirit
> into the wilderness, being tempted for forty days

by the devil. And in those days he ate nothing, and afterward, when they had ended, he was hungry. And the devil said to him, "If you are the Son of God, command this stone to become bread." Jesus answered him, saying, "It is written, 'man shall not live by bread alone, but by every word of God.'" Then the devil, taking him up on a high mountain, showed him all the kingdoms of the world in a moment of time. And the devil said to him, "All this authority I will give you, and their glory; for this has been delivered to me, and I give it to whomever I wish. Therefore, if you will worship before me, all will be yours." And Jesus answered and said to him, "Get behind me Satan! For it is written, 'You shall worship the Lord your God, and him only you shall serve.'" Then he brought him to Jerusalem, set him on the pinnacle of the temple, and said to him, "If you are the Son of God, throw yourself down from here. For it is written: 'He will give his angels charge over you, to keep you' and 'In their hands they shall bear you up, lest you dash your foot against a stone.'" And Jesus answered and said to him, "It has been said, 'You shall not tempt the LORD your God.'" Now when the devil had ended every temptation, he departed from him until an opportune time. Then Jesus returned in the power of the Spirit to Galilee,

Luke 4:1–14 (NKJV)

We see Satan came and tempted Jesus in the areas of the flesh. He appealed to the desire for gratification of the body's needs. He also tempted him to

walk by sight and not by faith, in testing the provision of God. Lastly, he tempted him to doubt he
was the Son of God, and offered him a shortcut in
obtaining Lordship over all kingdoms, without obedience to his Father. These are the temptations we
too must face.

> I write to you young men, because you are strong,
> and the word of God lives in you, and you have
> overcome the evil one. Do not love the world. If
> anyone loves the world, the love of the Father
> is not in him. For everything in the world—the
> cravings of sinful man, the lust of his eyes and
> the boasting of what he has and does—comes not
> from the Father but from the world. The world
> and its desires pass away, but the man who does
> the will of God lives forever.
>
> 1 John 2:14–17 (NIV)

The Spirit, as he leads us, will also allow us to go
into the wilderness and there we will decide whether
to serve God or our own sin. Until we can overcome
the desires of the flesh, we can never serve God
effectively. The decisions we make in the wilderness
will determine our success or failure in walking with
God. If we cannot resist temptation, every time God
has something good for us, Satan will come in the
area of our weakness and try to destroy it. The attack
of the devil will usually be in the area of our old sin
nature as long as he can defeat us there.

Let's look at the record of the nation Israel as
they were in the wilderness after Moses led them out
of Egypt. Sadly, we will see their defeat through their

refusal to obey God. They yielded to sin and believed in what they saw instead of believing by faith in what God had spoken to them.

> Moreover, brethren, I do not want you to be unaware that all our fathers were under the cloud, all passed through the sea, all were baptized into Moses in the cloud and in the sea, all ate the same spiritual food, and all drank the same spiritual drink. For they drank of that spiritual Rock that followed them, and that Rock was Christ. But with most of them God was not well pleased, for their bodies were scattered in the wilderness. Now these things became examples, to the intent that we should not lust after evil things as they also lusted. And do not become idolaters as were some of them. As it is written, "the people sat down to eat and drink, and rose up to play." Nor let us commit sexual immorality, as some of them did, and in one day twenty-three thousand fell; nor let us tempt Christ as some of them also tempted, and were destroyed by serpents; nor complain as some of them also complained, and were destroyed by the destroyer. Now all these things happened to them as examples, and they were written for our admonition, upon whom the ends of the ages have come. Therefore let him who thinks he stands take heed lest he fall.
>
> 1 Corinthians 10:1–12 (NIV)

The things that happened to the nation Israel in the wilderness serve as an example for us. That generation of Israel never came out of the wilderness, but died without obtaining their inheritance as a result of their disbelief. They were never able to overcome the temptation to sin.

If Jesus had given in to sin, I believe he would have never come out of the wilderness. If we give in to sin, we will remain in the wilderness fighting sin. Once Jesus overcame his temptation, he returned in the "power of the Spirit" (Luke 4:14) to Galilee. He then began his ministry of destroying the works of the devil, which ultimately led to his death on the cross, where he defeated Satan completely.

Our battle against sin is not a one-time event. We will fight our old sin nature and the devil's attacks until we leave this world. If and when we fail we must repent and know, "He who began the good work in us will complete it."

> Everyone who sins breaks the law; in fact, sin is lawlessness. But you know that he appeared so that he might take away our sins. And in him is no sin. No one who lives in him keeps on sinning. No one who continues to sin has either seen him or known him.
>
> 1 John 3:4–6 (NIV)

> My little children, these things I write to you, so that you may not sin. And if anyone sins, we have an advocate with the Father, Jesus Christ the righteous. And he himself is the propitiation for our sins, and not for ours only but also for the whole world.
>
> 1 John 2:1–2 (NKJV)

We, too, must overcome our sin before we can walk in the power of the Spirit. We must choose to say no to the invitation to sin by our own free-will. The temptation to sin comes to us through our fallen nature and the influence, or suggestion of the devil. We must never blame the devil for our own evil desires, and yet we must also understand that Satan is real and he comes to tempt us into sin. The Apostle Paul said in Galatians that those who are Christ have crucified the flesh with its affections. This is true, because if we haven't every time we try to follow Christ, Satan comes to us in the area of our weakness and stops us with sin.

Our decision to obey the Word and say no to sin must be solid and unwavering if we are to know victory and power in Christ. In order to do this, we must be careful to continually ask ourselves; Am I in prayer? Am I in the Word? Am I in fellowship? Am I giving? Am I sharing my faith? Am I in praise and worship? The same as we need to eat and sleep to remain strong physically we also need to do the things I just listed to remain strong in the Lord and free from sin. Once we are free from sin, we are free to say yes to the invitation to join God's army as a Holy Warrior!

When you have died to sin and self and begin to seek only his glory, there will be a time when you will experience a change in your heart. As you spend time in his presence you begin to feel what was in the heart of the Father when he sent his Son to suffer and die so we might know life. The more we experience this selfless love, the more we too become willing to forsake our own comfort and increase, so that we can share his Salvation with those who are still in the dark. We see this heart attitude in what Paul wrote:

> Yet indeed I also count all things loss for the excellence of the knowledge of Christ Jesus my Lord, for whom I have suffered the loss of all things, and count them as rubbish, that I may gain Christ and be found in him, not having my own righteousness, which is from the law, but that which is through faith in Christ, the righteousness which is from God by faith; that I may know him and the power of his resurrection, and the fellowship of his sufferings, being conformed to his death.
>
> Philippians 3:8–10 (NKJV)

With painful memories of previous battles lost, the wounds I have received and sorrow in my heart for past comrades that have fallen I need to tell you: if you are going to bring forth a fruit that remains from your life as a disciple you must go to war. If you just want to be saved and know the gifts and goodness of God, that's okay; but if you really do want to be a disciple and see fruit, you too must take up your cross and share in the fellowship of his sufferings.

> They preached the good news in that city and won a large number of disciples, then they returned to Lystra, Iconium and Antioch, strengthening the

disciples and encouraging them to remain true to the faith. "We must go through many hardships to enter the kingdom of God."

Acts 14:22 (NIV)

There is an example of the army of God in the account of David and Goliath found in 1 Samuel 17, where we read of how the army of Israel (army of God) was encamped against the Philistines (army of darkness). Every day, Goliath, would come out and challenge the army of Israel and then go back to his side. Satan was satisfied to allow the army of God to camp and pretend they were in the battle as long as they sat there and pretended they were at war, because he knew he possessed their inheritance. He also knew until they stood up and by faith began to come against him he would continue to occupy what God had given to them. Oh, how many people both pastor and congregation are deceived into believing that discipleship without confrontation and attack is going to gain victory.

Our calling is to not only be sanctified and know victory for ourselves, but it is also to advance the kingdom of God out into the darkness of this present world and reclaim others who are lost. To be effective in this fight of faith we need to understand that our battle is not against flesh and blood, but against Satan and his kingdom. This means we do not fight on the carnal level. Instead, we fight in the realm of the spirit. This involves a different type of warfare than we are used to.

> For though we live in the world, we do not wage
> war as the world does. The weapons we fight with
> are not the weapons of the world. On the contrary,
> they have divine power to demolish strongholds.
>
> 2 Corinthians 10:4 (NIV)

The victory of our faith is realized as we walk a life free from sin, disciplined in Bible study, prayer, confession, and worship.

I have already shared with you how important prayer and the Word are, but you need to be aware of the importance of confession and worship in your battle against the enemy. When we confess our authority in Christ, it puts the world, the spirit realms, and even ourselves "on notice" that we belong to God and stand triumphant in Christ. While we are praying and fasting, we many times turn the battle by our confession, whether negative to defeat, or positive in faith to victory. Anytime we begin to doubt God and what he has done or is doing, or will do in the future, we need to confess aloud to ourselves and to others what a mighty God we serve. Our confession must stay in agreement with the Word. It is by releasing our faith through our speaking that we allow God to be the God; who is more than able to accomplish all we ask and hope for. As we worship him for who he is and his goodness to us; we defeat the realms of darkness that are against us. As we speak out the Word, confess our authority in Christ, and walk in praise and worship, we overcome the enemy and his intentions for us.

Be careful of anyone who is using any of the devil's methods in relating to others. They all appeal to the flesh and it's easy to be deceived by the adversary. Some of the methods Satan uses against us are deception, fear, intimidation, flattery, manipulation, seduction, procrastination, depression, and others. He is not only evil he is also willing to use every evil practice and person against us to stop all God has for us. He does not fight fair, and is subtle in his allusions as he seeks our destruction.

This will become clearer to you as you live your discipleship in the days ahead. You will discover the devil is not only busy trying to destroy your personal faith, but he is also at work in the church. We can identify Satan and his false workers by the way they live, the methods they use and the fruit they bear.

All of this should not move us as we walk in love by faith. We know God has ordained the church (the Body of Christ) of which we are now a part to show forth his glory and destroy the works of the devil. We have been ordained to live in this spiritual arena and to bring forth much fruit that remains. Jesus said he would build his church and the gates of hell would not prevail against it. The good news is we are on the winning team!

The Great Commission

I remember so well in the beginning of my walk with God, how I came to realize the relationship I had found with Jesus was what the whole world was searching for! I began to be burdened with the need to share the message of his love. I soon found I not only had a desire to do this, but Jesus had actually commissioned (sent) me to do so as a member of his church.

> And Jesus came up and spoke to them saying, "All authority has been given me in heaven and on earth. Go therefore and make disciples of all the nations, baptizing them in the name of the Father and the Son and the Holy Spirit, teaching them to observe all that I commanded you; and lo, I am with you always, even to the end of the age."
>
> Matthew 28:18–20 (NAS)

And these signs shall follow those who believe: In my name they will cast out demons; they will speak with new tongues; they will take up serpents; and if they drink anything deadly, it will by no means hurt them; they will lay hands on the sick, and they will recover.

Mark 16:17–18 (NKJV)

And you will be witnesses in Jerusalem, and in all Judea and Samaria, and to the ends of the earth.

Acts 1:8 (NIV)

We are to begin telling others about Jesus, first where we are here and now, then to those close by and then on to the ends of the earth. We find preaching the good news (the Gospel) was the focus of the early church in the days following Jesus' return to heaven at the end of his ministry here on earth:

Peter replied, "repent and be baptized, every one of you, in the name of Jesus Christ for the forgiveness of your sins" ... with many other words he warned them; and he pleaded with them, "Save yourselves from this corrupt generation." Those who accepted his message were baptized, and about three thousand were added to their number that day.

Acts 2:38, 40–41 (NIV)

Those who had been scattered preached the word where ever they went.

Acts 4 (NIV)

For after that in the wisdom of God the world
by wisdom knew not God, it pleased God by the
foolishness of preaching to save them that believe.

1 Corinthians 1:21 (KJV)

Every believer needs to be involved in proclaim-
ing the message of Salvation. First we must always
be ready to personally share (give an account) of our
faith to others. Secondly, we must be a part of the
united effort of the church to take this "Good News"
to the ends of the earth. The Apostle Paul wrote in
his letter to the church at Rome:

How then will they call on him in who they have
not believed? And how shall they believe in him
of who they have not heard? And how shall they
hear without a preacher? And how shall they
preach, except they be sent? As it is written, how
beautiful are the feet of them that preach the
gospel of peace, and bring glad tidings of good
things.

Romans 10:14–15 (KJV)

Let's never be deceived into believing God has
already predetermined who will be saved and those
who won't. The scripture tells us this isn't true.

The Lord is not slow in keeping his promise, as
some understand slowness, he is patient with you,
not wanting anyone to perish, but everyone to
come to repentance.

II Peter 3:9 (NIV)

First of all then, I urge that supplications, prayers, intercessions be made for all men ... this is good, and it is acceptable in the sight of God our Savior, who desires all men to be saved and to come to the knowledge of the truth.

1Timothy 2:1, 3–4 (RSV)

I want to encourage you to not hesitate in beginning to share your faith at every opportunity! We all have a tendency to find excuses for not doing so. We know the time is now.

Do you not say, "There are yet four months, then comes the harvest? I tell you, lift up your eyes, and see how the fields are already white for harvest. He who reaps receives wages, and gathers fruit for eternal life."

John 4:35–36 (RSV)

I can honestly say from my own experience, when we are faithful in sharing the Gospel, we will find ourselves introducing many others to Jesus Christ. I will be praying for you to have great success in reaching lost souls for him.

The Finish

As I have been telling you these things, I have had a burden to somehow help you to see the finish of your walk of faith in Jesus. As we live our lives in an ever deepening relationship with the Lord, we need to know we will one day forever be in his presence. This should be our motivation and goal all the days of our lives. This expectation should never be far from our minds. There will be many other glorious moments along the way as we go from victory to victory, but nothing must ever supersede our goal of being with him forever.

> After this I looked and there before me was a great multitude that no one could count, from every nation, tribe, people and language, standing before the throne and in front of the Lamb. They were wearing white robes and were holding palm branches in their hands. And they cried out in a

loud voice: "Salvation belongs to our God who sits on the throne, and to the Lamb."

Revelation 7:9–10 (NIV)

For the Lamb at the center of the throne will be their shepherd; he will lead them to springs of living water. And God will wipe away every tear.

Revelation 7:17 (NIV)

The reason this is such a burden to me is I have seen so many fall along the way. Jesus said in Matthew 7:14 (NIV): "But small is the gate and narrow the road that leads to life, and only a few find it."

When our vision begins to drift, so does our walk; and if we are not careful, we will become disillusioned in our life of faith. There are times as we walk with God, he will do things in ways that do not meet our expectations and move in ways we do not understand. Many times, it will appear in the natural that what we believe and hope for is never going to happen and simply isn't true. We must never doubt God and his unfathomable love for us! This can cause us to doubt and no longer trust. Our doubts bring disbelief and disbelief brings sin. Sin brings death, and we never see all God has for us. We must deliberately fix our mind and vision on the love and faithfulness of God in heaven. Romans 8:28 assures us God is in control: "And we know that all things work together for good to those who love God, to those who are the called according to his purpose." (NKJV) We must relate to life with an eternal perspective.

When our vision shifts, so does the outcome of

our footsteps. Our vision must be home in heaven with our Lord. Our discipleship can never focus on how hard the journey is, how high the cost, or even his blessings of today. Let's read Hebrews 12:1–4 (KJV):

> Wherefore seeing we also are compassed about with so great a cloud of witnesses, let us lay aside every weight, and the sin which doth so easily beset us, and let us run with patience the race that is set before us. Looking unto Jesus, the author and finisher of our faith; who for the joy set before him endured the cross, despising the shame, and is set down at the right hand of the throne of God. For consider him that endured such contradiction of sinners against himself, lest you be wearied and faint in your minds. You have not yet resisted unto blood, striving against sin.

We see from this passage, the way Jesus endured the cross. He did so by focusing his faith on the future day when he would again be in heaven in the presence of his Father. He was looking ahead to the joy he would know when you and I received him as our Savior. We, too, must fix our vision on the joy set before us if we are to overcome in our walk of faith. If we aren't careful we will yield in our mind to what is against us in the natural, instead of being steady in our faith in what we know, but cannot see. It is my fervent prayer for both of us, we can one day say as Paul:

> For I am now ready to be offered, and the time of my departure is at hand. I have fought a good

fight, I have finished my course, I have kept the faith: Henceforth there is laid up for me a crown of righteousness, which the Lord, the righteous judge, shall give me at that day: and not to me only, but unto all them also that love his appearing.

II Timothy 4:6–8 (KJV)

We must keep an eternal perspective with heaven as our goal, because the road between here and there at times isn't easy. This isn't a life of leisure we've been born into, but a fight of faith where nobody fights fair on the other side. If we don't have a clear vision of ourselves walking down those streets of gold in fellowship with our Lord Jesus, we will never make it.

Our vision is on eternity. That's why living won't make sense if we look at it from a temporal perspective only. If what other people think of us, our retirement, the place we live, or anything else means more to us than our place in heaven; we will fall short of God's best for us. I know this sounds harsh, but it's what the Bible says. If we are going to know all the reward God has for us, we need to be steady in our belief of our standing in Christ and where we are going.

To continue immovable in our walk as a disciple we need to know one day we will stand before God to be judged and rewarded for our life here on earth. Let's look now at a few scriptures:

But I do not want you to be ignorant, brethren, concerning those who have fallen asleep, lest you sorrow as others who have no hope. For if we believe that Jesus died and rose again, even so God will bring with him those who sleep in Jesus. For this we say to you by the word of the Lord, that we who are alive and remain until the coming of the Lord will by no means precede those who are asleep. For the Lord himself will descend from heaven with a shout, with the voice of an archangel and with the trumpet of God. And the dead in Christ will rise first. Then we who are alive and remain shall be caught up together with them in the clouds to meet the Lord in the air. And thus we shall always be with the Lord. Therefore comfort one another with these words.

1 Thessalonians 4:13–18 (NKJV)

"Do not be amazed at this, for a time is coming when all who are in their grave will hear his voice and come out—those who have done good will rise to live, and those who have done evil will rise to be condemned."

John 5:28–29 (NIV)

And it is appointed for men to die once, but after this the judgment.

Hebrews 9:27 (NKJV)

The Word tells us the first judgment all men must face is the White Throne judgment. This is where we will be judged in regard to our acceptance or rejection of Jesus. We read about this in the book of Revelation, chapter 20:11–12, 14–15 (NIV):

Then I saw a great white throne and him who was seated on it. Earth and sky fled from his presence, and there was no place for them. And I saw the dead, great and small, standing before the throne, and books were opened. Another book was opened, which is the book of life. The dead were judged according to what they had done... Then death and Hades were thrown into the lake of fire. The lake of fire is the second death. If anyone's name was not found written in the Book of Life, he was thrown into the lake of fire.

The Bible shows us those who have received Jesus and have their names written in the Lamb's Book of Life will pass on from the White Throne Judgment to the judgment seat of Christ. We will be judged there to determine our rewards, not on whether we get to go to heaven. Think about the following scriptures.

Then they that feared the LORD spoke often one to another; and the Lord hearkened, and heard it, and a book of remembrance was written before him for them that feared the LORD, and that thought upon his name. And they shall be mine, saith the LORD of hosts, in that day when I make up my jewels; and I will spare them, as a man spareth his own son that serveth him. Then shall ye return, and discern between the righteous and the wicked, between him that serveth God and him that serveth him not. For, behold the day cometh, that shall burn like an oven; and all the proud, yea, and all that do wickedly, shall be stubble; and the day that cometh shall burn them up, saith the

LORD of hosts, that is shall leave them neither root nor branch. But unto you that fear my name shall the sun of righteousness rise with healing in his wings; and ye shall go forth, and grow up like calves of the stall.

Malachi 3:16–4:3 (KJV)

For no one can lay any foundation other than the one already laid, which is Jesus Christ. If any man builds on this foundation using gold, silver, costly stones, wood, hay or straw, his work will be shown for what it is, because the Day will bring it to light. It will be revealed with fire, and the fire will test the quality of each man's work. If what he has built survives, he will receive his reward. If it is burned up, he will suffer loss; he himself will be saved, but only as one escaping through the flames.

1 Corinthians 3:11 (NIV)

"He who receives you receives Me, and he who receives Me receives him who sent me. He who receives a prophet in the name of a prophet shall receive a prophet's reward … And whoever gives one of these little ones only a cup of cold water in the name of a disciple, assuredly, I say to you he shall by no means lose his reward.

Matthew 10:40–42 (NKJV)

Blessed are you when men hate you, and when they exclude you, and revile you, and cast out your name as evil, for the Son of Man's sake. Rejoice in that day and leap for joy! For indeed your reward is great in heaven.

Luke 6:22–23 (NKJV)

As you study the Word, you will also see there are special crowns promised to various ones, such as the over-comers, the elders, the martyrs, and the righteous. The Apostle Paul spoke of his desire to one-day stand before his King and to be rewarded with a crown.

> Do you not know that in a race all the runners run, but only one gets the prize? Run in such a way as to get the prize. Everyone who competes in the games goes into strict training. They do it to get a crown that will not last; but we do it to get a crown that will last forever. Therefore I do not run like a man running aimlessly; I do no fight like a man beating the air. No, I beat my body and make it my slave so that after I have preached to others, I myself will not be disqualified for the prize.
>
> 1 Corinthians 9:24–27 (NIV)

After the judgment seat of Christ, we will enter heaven to be in the presence of our God forever and ever.

> Then I saw a new heaven and a new earth, for the first heaven and the first earth had passed away, and there was no longer any sea. I saw the Holy City, the New Jerusalem, coming down out of heaven from God, prepared as a bride beautifully dressed for her husband. And I heard a loud voice from the throne saying, "Now the dwelling of God is with men, and he will live with them, they will be his people, and God himself will be with them and be their God. He will wipe every

tear from their eyes. There will be no more death or mourning or crying or pain, for the old order of things has passed away."

Revelation 21:1–4 (NIV)

"They are before the throne of God and serve him day and night in his temple; and he who sits on the throne will spread his tent over them. Never again will they hunger; never again will they thirst. The sun will not beat upon them, nor any scorching heart."

Revelation 7:15–16 (NIV)

And the nations of those who are saved shall walk in its light, and the kings of the earth bring their glory and honor into it. Its gates shall not be shut at all by day (there will be no night there). And they shall bring the glory and the honor of the nations into it. But there shall by no means enter it anything that defiles, or causes an abomination or a lie, but only those who are written in the Lamb's Book of Life.

Revelation 21:24–27 (NKJV)

Then the angel showed me the river of the water of life, as clear as crystal, flowing from the throne of God and of the Lamb down the middle of the great street of the City. On each side of the river stood the Tree of Life, bearing twelve crops of fruit, yielding its fruit every month. And the leaves of the tree are for the healing of the nations. No longer will there be any curse. The throne of God and of the Lamb will be in the city, and his servants will serve him. They will see his face, and his name will be on their foreheads. There will be no more night. They will not need the light of a lamp or the light of the sun, for the Lord God will give them light. And they will reign forever and ever.

Revelation 22:1–5 (NIV)

I know I have just given you a lot of scripture pertaining to what we will obtain after we pass from this life. Oh, the joy of serving God and being with him forever. I hope you never allow anything to cause this to dim in your heart as you follow on to walk with him.

Jesus Christ, who is the faithful witness, the first-born from the dead, and the ruler of the kings of the earth. To him who loves us and has freed us from our sins by his blood, and has made us to be a kingdom and priests to serve his God and Father—to him be glory and power forever and ever. Amen

Revelation 1:5–6 (NIV)

Closing

It has been so wonderful to be able to have this time together with you throughout these pages. I hope you have enjoyed it as much as I have. In closing, my friend, I would like to pray with you:

Dear Lord, how can I thank you enough for your gift of eternal life? I only have praise and worship in my heart and on my lips for you. Now I see I am on an incredible journey with you that will never end. I confess I am so inadequate at being your disciple. My deepest desire is to become more like you every day and in every way. Please help me to know a relationship with you, through the Holy Spirit, as I seek to live for you and you alone. Please walk beside me, hold my hand, and pick me back up when I fail or fall. I lay my life before you and ask you to be my Lord from this day forward, until I kneel before your throne in eternity.

In your name, Jesus, I pray.

Amen.